DOES GOD CARE ABOUT ME?

*Psalm 73 on
Doubt and Distress
in the Christian Life*

Gordon J. Keddie

**SCOTTISH REFORMED HERITAGE
PUBLICATIONS
2023**

© Scottish Reformed Heritage Publications, 2023

First Published in 2023 by
Scottish Reformed Heritage Publications,
19 Newton Park, Kirkhill, Inverness-shire, IV5 7QB.

All rights reserved. No part of this book may be reproduced, stored in a retrieval system, or transmitted, in any form or by any means (electronic, mechanical, photocopying, recording, or otherwise) without the prior written permission of the publisher.

ISBN **978-1-4466-5050-9**

Unless otherwise indicated Scripture quotes are from the 1982 edition of the *New King James Version,* Thomas Nelson, Inc.

Cover Art:
The Parable of the Rich Fool by Rembrandt (1627). (Luke 12:13-21). Gemäldegalerie, Berlin. Original image by Rembrandt. Uploaded by Mark Cartwright, published on 19 February 2019. The copyright holder has published this content under the following license: Public Domain. This item is in the public domain, and can be used, copied, and modified without any restrictions.

Note:

This present volume on Psalm 73 – *Does God Care About Me?* – was checked and approved by the author before his passing on 19th May 2023. It was proof-read and set up by Michael Bushell and prepared by him for publication. Sincere thanks are due to Michael for all his work in this connection.

Towards the end of his life, the author wished me, his younger brother, to be involved with the final production, together with Michael Bushell. Consequently, I have added an Appreciation by way of a brief biographical sketch of my brother for inclusion with the work. As a result, the book is being distributed under the imprint of Scottish Reformed Heritage Publications.

John W. Keddie

TABLE OF CONTENTS

Rev. Gordon James Keddie (1944-2023) – An Appreciation   5

PREFACE   9

Psalm 73   11

PART ONE: DOUBTS   13

Chapter 1 Does God Really Care?   15

PART TWO: DISTRESS AND DEVASTATION   27

Chapter 2 Think It Through   29

Chapter 3 Grasping The Real Issue   39

Chapter 4 Grieving Your Guilt   49

PART THREE: DELIVERANCE   55

Chapter 5 Grace   57

Chapter 6 Growth   63

Chapter 7 The Desire of Your Heart   73

Chapter 8 The Strength of Your Heart   79

Chapter 9 Draw Near to God   85

PUBLICATIONS BY THE AUTHOR   95

Rev. Gordon James Keddie (1944-2023)

An Appreciation

My late brother, Gordon Keddie, respected minister in the Reformed Presbyterian Church of North America (RPCNA), entered his eternal rest on 19th May 2023. He passed away at his home in Greenwood, Indiana, in his 79th year, having suffered illness for several years. He was a faithful preacher of the gospel of Jesus Christ and a prolific author of popular evangelical and reformed expository commentaries.

Born and brought up in Edinburgh, Scotland, Gordon Keddie's upbringing was churchy but nominal (the local Church of Scotland). He traced his spiritual change to hearing a gospel sermon from Ecclesiastes 12:1 as a 17-year-old on 20th May 1962. This was at a Scripture Union rally in the borders' town of Galashiels. At that point he was a pupil at George Heriot's School in Edinburgh. Shortly afterwards he went up to study for a BSc degree in Zoology at Aberdeen University. (In his volume on Ecclesiastes, *Looking for the Good Life*, first published in 1991, he describes his experience movingly on pages 164-165 of that first edition).

In Aberdeen Gordon became attached to Gilcomston South Church of Scotland, then under the faithful ministry of the Rev. William Still. The influence of Mr Still's preaching was evident throughout his own subsequent ministry. It also had an indirect influence on me. Through my brother's witness, I came to profess saving faith in Christ in 1966, having been encouraged to attend the ministry of the Rev. James Phillip at Holyrood Abbey Church of Scotland in Edinburgh, of which I became a communicant member in 1966.

After graduation in 1966 Gordon subsequently undertook teacher-training in Edinburgh (DipEd) and for 3 years (1967-1970) taught biology and physics at Trinity Academy in Leith. By then we had re-evaluated our attachment to the Church of Scotland and moved to the Free Church of Scotland, one of the smaller confessional presbyterian and reformed churches in Scotland. At that point Gordon felt a desire to learn more of the Reformed faith and decided to take a ThM course at Westminster Theological Seminary in Philadelphia in 1970. Whilst at Seminary he felt a call to the ministry of the Word and after a year at the Reformed Presbyterian Seminary in Pittsburgh (1972-73) and another year at

Westminster, he was called to the congregation of North Hills Reformed Presbyterian Church in Pittsburgh. That was in June 1974, the month following his marriage to Jane McMillan, daughter of a Reformed Presbyterian minister. (Gordon's passing was the day after their 49th wedding anniversary). In the course of time three sons were born to them: Donald, Iain and David. At the time of his passing Gordon and Jane had three beloved grandchildren by David and his wife, Christina. Iain and his wife, Erin, were expecting their first child. (Eoin James Keddie was safely delivered on 29th September 2023).

Gordon was 7½ years at North Hills but felt a strong pull to return to his native Scotland and, although he became a Free Church minister without a charge for 2 years, after supplying Scottish RP congregations for a couple of years, in 1986 he returned to the USA and the Reformed Presbyterian Church of North America to minister in the State College congregation in Pennsylvania. In his 18 years there the congregation grew from a 'church plant', to become a viable congregation. But in 2004 he received a call to Southside RPCNA congregation in Indianapolis, in which he spent 10 challenging but happy years during which the congregation grew, so that the church building had to be enlarged. He retired from the pastoral ministry there after exactly 10 years, in his 70th year, in 2014.

It was whilst in Scotland (1981-1986) that my brother began his writing ministry. The bulk of it emerged from his preaching, as he put into print expository sermon series. It started with his book on Judges and Ruth (*Even in Darkness*) first published by Evangelical Press in 1985. Reaction to this volume ensured that he would be under pressure to provide more. And he did. Between 1985 and 1993 he produced another 7 commentaries in the Evangelical Press 'Welwyn' series, a number of which went into several printings and were translated into foreign languages. A reviewer of his work on Ecclesiastes (*Looking for the Good Life*, Presbyterian & Reformed, 1991), writing in 1992, was to comment that, "Gordon Keddie is fast gaining a most deserved reputation as one of the most helpful Reformed commentators today" (Peter Barnes). A feature of his expository work was that he seemed every bit at home in studies in the Old Testament as he was in the New Testament. His largest writing project was a 2-volume study 'Study Commentary' on the gospel according to John, amounting to 956 pages (Evangelical Press, 2001).

In his retirement he kept busy with his writing, and it is believed that volumes on Romans and 1 and 2 Corinthians will be forthcoming from

Crown & Covenant Publications. Besides such expository works he was also responsible for other doctrinal and devotional pieces, as well as collections of early Reformed Presbyterian forefathers in the faith, and numerous articles for magazines and journals. The book that perhaps gave him most pleasure was his volume on *Prayers of the Bible* (Crown & Covenant, 2017, 764pages). This comprised 366 daily Devotionals 'to encourage your prayer life.' In some ways Gordon reflected the statement in Psalm 45, both in relation to his preaching and writing: "My heart is indicting a good matter: I speak of the things which I have made touching the king: my tongue is the pen of a ready writer" (v1). This present volume on Psalm 73 was prepared for publication just before his passing. Gordon has no doubt left a goodly legacy for the Reformed and Evangelical constituency.

Despite his evident writing and preaching gifts, Gordon was a diffident character who had no aspirations either to academia, or conference speaking, though he had ability in both these areas. His passion was preaching the unsearchable riches of Christ. For the greater part his books were simply an extension of his preaching ministry. They are full of sound doctrine, homiletics, pastoral theology, and illustrative material. In privately circulated personal 'Reminiscences' he put this in perspective in 2021:

> Many years ago, the late Bruce Stewart (then President of the RP Theol. Seminary in Pittsburgh), commenting on my early rather prolific writing at the time, expressed the thought I was maybe more interested in writing than preaching. That, after a short review, made me realize that my top interest was truly the preaching of the Word of God, and that writing was no more than an aid to the great goal of Biblical preaching – the salvation of souls and nurture of Christian lives in practical discipleship. It is the "foolishness of preaching" by which God is pleased to "save them that believe" and disseminate His wisdom in an unwise world (1 Cor. 1:21). That also must be the abiding concern and commitment of all who would seek to serve the work of the Lord in the world! Against this, writing – useful as it is in itself – can only at best be regarded as a lesser tool and a minor privilege for any of God's servants.

This is an appropriate ending in an appreciation of the person and work of my brother. Meantime we face the telling truth of Ecclesiastes: "For man goes to his eternal home, and the mourners go about the streets" (12:5).

It is hard to overstate how much I owe personally to my brother in my life. We were brothers in two ways: in the flesh and in the Spirit. My own interest in Christian faith and life was initiated and constantly encouraged by him from when I came to faith in Christ. A man of clear thinking and understanding of Reformed Christian doctrine, faith and life, Gordon was a consistent, faithful, and fruitful servant of his Saviour to the end. He was sympathetic and tireless, yet he possessed a notable wit and humour; and was a great conversationalist. He will be missed. His wife, Jane, was a great helpmeet to Gordon over 49 years of marriage and he delighted in his sons, daughters-in-law, and grandchildren. He will also be missed by his own church, and by the wider Reformed Churches too. Ultimately the most important thing that anyone can say is what the Apostle Paul wrote in one place: "For to me to live is Christ, and to die is gain" (Phil. 1:21). That, certainly, was Gordon's conviction. As he wrote in this work on Psalm 73, published here for the first time: "How much more will we glory in the Lord in prospect of soon being with Him in Glory? O, think often of Heaven. We are not long here. And strive earnestly for Heaven, and you will be all the more blessed on Earth." It is poignant to think that these were among the last words he wrote in this world.

A funeral service was held in Southside Reformed Presbyterian Church on Friday, 26 May (2023), in which two sons spoke feelingly of their father and his faith and influence, and his former assistant pastor, David Whitla, preached a fine sermon on Psalm 73. The following day his mortal remains were laid to rest in the Reformed Presbyterian Cemetery at New Galilee, Pennsylvania. On the question: 'What benefits do believers receive from Christ at death?' the *Shorter Catechism* answers beautifully and hopefully: 'The souls of believers are at their death made perfect in holiness and do immediately pass into glory; and their bodies, being still united to Christ, do rest in their graves till the resurrection.' "Until the day break and the shadows flee away."

John W. Keddie,
Kirkhill,
Inverness-shire,
Scotland.

November 2023

Gordon Keddie in the pulpit

PREFACE

EVERYBODY knows that the world is corrupt and blighted with wickedness. The fact that we remark on honesty and are surprised by kindness just proves the point. A corollary to this is that the corrupt and the dishonest – people with plastic integrity – often do rather well and get away with their corruption, while the upright are not infrequently at a serious disadvantage. "I have seen the wicked in great power," says the Psalmist, "and spreading himself like a green bay tree." (Psalm 37:35 KJV).

This makes many a Christian think, "Why does God let the wicked prosper? Is He really in control? Does He care – about justice, goodness and truth – and does He truly care about *me*?" It may seem sometimes that God is not doing what we expect Him to be doing – like observably punishing the wicked and rewarding the righteous. And if you are going through a hard time, you might ask, "Why do I have to go through such a struggle?" Or perhaps you just see God's people – visibly godly people – struggling and oppressed, while the ungodly happily sin their way to fame and fortune?

This is what the seventy-third Psalm is about – our stumbling, even "losing it," over the apparent success and prosperity of those who clearly despise the Lord. The psalmist, Asaph,[1] looks back on how this seemingly

---

[1] There has long been debate as to who this Asaph was; whether the singer of David's day (1 Chr. 6:39), the seer of Hezekiah's time (2 Chr. 29:30; Neh. 12:46), or, one belonging to the school of Asaph, otherwise unnamed (*cf.* 2 Kings 18:18, 37; Neh. 2:8; 11:17). Psalms 73 and 74 are the first two in Book III of the Psalms (i.e., Psalms 73-89). In #73, the Psalmist reflects on his individual distress, while in #74, the focus is on the corporate distress of the nation over the depredations of the invading enemy. Whether these are written by the same "Asaph" is not clear. The material point is that both are written by someone called "Asaph," who writes under divine inspiration, the former about his experience of personal doubt, devastation and deliverance, and the latter lamenting the devastating consequences of the apostasy of the people of God. Most of the Book III Psalms are in the vein of the sorrows of God's people in the face of the Babylonian invasion of 596 BC. In spite of the assertion that the individual perspective of Psalm 73 cannot be that of the Asaph of David's day, centuries earlier, it does not follow that this was not included by the later editor to connect with an intimate record of personal devastation already long established in the Word of God and the piety of God's covenant people (*cf.* O. Palmer Robertson, *The Flow of the Psalms* (Phillipsburg, NJ, P&R: 2015), 125). Whichever "Asaph" penned Psalm 73, it is certain that this is one of the great gems of Scripture for the understanding of personal doubt and devastation in the lives of believers – and not least the deliverance effected by God's saving grace as promised and proclaimed in His Word.

[9]

perennial state of affairs nearly took the rug out from under his faith as he was tempted to doubt if God really cares – assuming He is really there at all! He doubted God and was desperately discouraged. His faith was shaken. Self-pity crushed his spirit. He was devasted in his heart and soul, and he entertained unbelief. He just could not fathom what God was up to in all of this. Confusion reigned in his soul.

Doubts, and discouragements tend to dog, and sometimes devastate, the most stable of people in this fallen world, whatever their "faith" may be – or the lack of it. And this is not an uncommon experience in the lives of God's people who are consciously and sincerely trusting and resting on the covenant promises of God as laid out in the Scriptures and, indeed enjoyed in personal faith in their Savior Jesus. To this reality, Psalm 73 explains and applies the countervailing truth that the Lord truly is good to His people, such that if their feet are slipping toward letting go of the Lord, He is not going to let go of those who truly belong to Him and will, in Christ, "walk by faith," and "not by sight" (2 Cor. 5:7).

The arrangement of this Psalm begins with the affirmation of the basic irreducible truth of God's goodness (v. 1), which the Psalmist had previously doubted and which he goes on to discuss in the first half of the psalm (vv. 2-14). He then turns to how this impacted his thinking – and, indeed, the state of his soul. He was devastated by what he saw he had come to – and when he properly understood the actual condition and eternal destiny of the godless (vv. 15-21). Through this exposure of his sinfulness, the Lord, in His amazing grace, delivers him by humbling him, wonderfully restoring his soul, and renewing his trust in, dependance upon, and fellowship with his reconciled Father in Heaven (vv. 22-26). The Psalm concludes with the Psalmist's commitment to the complete reversal of his backsliding from the Lord. The feet that were formerly slipping return to solid ground, and the heart that embarked upon the repudiation of his trust in the Lord, again drew near to God with the commitment to trust Him and bear witness to all His works (vv. 27-28). The implications and invitations are so clear: "He who has ears to hear, let him hear!" (Matt. 11:15).

Gordon J. Keddie,
Greenwood,
Indiana, USA.

PSALM 73

¹ A Psalm of Asaph. Truly God is good to Israel, To such as are pure in heart. ² But as for me, my feet had almost stumbled; My steps had nearly slipped. ³ For I was envious of the boastful, When I saw the prosperity of the wicked. ⁴ For there are no pangs in their death, But their strength is firm. ⁵ They are not in trouble as other men, Nor are they plagued like other men. ⁶ Therefore pride serves as their necklace; Violence covers them like a garment. ⁷ Their eyes bulge with abundance; They have more than heart could wish. ⁸ They scoff and speak wickedly concerning oppression; They speak loftily. ⁹ They set their mouth against the heavens, And their tongue walks through the earth. ¹⁰ Therefore his people return here, And waters of a full cup are drained by them. ¹¹ And they say, "How does God know? And is there knowledge in the Most High?" ¹² Behold, these are the ungodly, Who are always at ease; They increase in riches.

¹³ Surely I have cleansed my heart in vain, And washed my hands in innocence. ¹⁴ For all day long I have been plagued, And chastened every morning. ¹⁵ If I had said, "I will speak thus," Behold, I would have been untrue to the generation of Your children. ¹⁶ When I thought how to understand this, It was too painful for me— ¹⁷ Until I went into the sanctuary of God; Then I understood their end. ¹⁸ Surely You set them in slippery places; You cast them down to destruction. ¹⁹ Oh, how they are brought to desolation, as in a moment! They are utterly consumed with terrors. ²⁰ As a dream when one awakes, So, Lord, when You awake, You shall despise their image.

²¹ Thus my heart was grieved, And I was vexed in my mind. ²² I was so foolish and ignorant; I was like a beast before You. ²³ Nevertheless I am continually with You; You hold me by my right hand. ²⁴ You will guide me with Your counsel, And afterward receive me to glory. ²⁵ Whom have I in heaven but You? And there is none upon earth that I desire besides You. ²⁶ My flesh and my heart fail; But God is the strength of my heart and my portion forever. ²⁷ For indeed, those who are far from You shall perish; You have destroyed all those who desert You for harlotry. ²⁸ But it is good for me to draw near to God; I have put my trust in the Lord God, That I may declare all Your works.

PART ONE

DOUBTS

Psalm 73:1-14

Chapter 1

Does God Really Care?

Truly God is good to Israel, To such as are pure in heart. ² But as for me, my feet had almost stumbled; My steps had nearly slipped. ³ For I was envious of the boastful, When I saw the prosperity of the wicked. ⁴ For there are no pangs in their death, But their strength is firm. ⁵ They are not in trouble as other men, Nor are they plagued like other men. ⁶ Therefore pride serves as their necklace; Violence covers them like a garment. ⁷ Their eyes bulge with abundance; They have more than heart could wish. ⁸ They scoff and speak wickedly concerning oppression; They speak loftily. ⁹ They set their mouth against the heavens, And their tongue walks through the earth. ¹⁰ Therefore his people return here, And waters of a full cup are drained by them. ¹¹ And they say, "How does God know? And is there knowledge in the Most High?" ¹² Behold, these are the ungodly, Who are always at ease; They increase in riches. ¹³ Surely I have cleansed my heart in vain, And washed my hands in innocence. ¹⁴ For all day long I have been plagued, And chastened every morning.
(Psalm 73:1-14)

The Scots pastor, Andrew A. Bonar, describes the topic of this psalm as "Messiah's people almost offended in Him."[2] Even John the Baptizer had entertained a certain doubt about Jesus, perhaps because Jesus had not brought in God's Kingdom as he thought the Messiah should. John's feet arguably came close to stumbling, but the Lord kept him on solid ground with the encouragement – equally applicable to all of us – "Blessed is he who is not offended because of Me." (Luke 7:23). When the world is manifestly unfair, and if God Himself seems to be unfair to us, and we feel our feet stumbling and our steps slipping (73:2), we may well be tempted to think that the Lord is far away – a *deus absconditus*. You can see how Asaph's psalm is for us all, for it is clearly designed to bring us back from

---

[2] Andrew A. Bonar, *Christ and His Church in the Book of Psalms* (New York: Carter, 1860), 221.

the precipice of any doubt and practical unbelief with which we may be wrestling.

What Do I Really Believe?
*Truly God is good to Israel,
to such as are pure in heart. (Psalm 73:1)*

Asaph was wrestling with nagging personal doubt over God's love for him and His sovereignty over adverse circumstances. Doubt in the living God and in God's truth is bound to be dangerous. Asaph came to realize that he needed a cure for the temptation to question the faithfulness of God and the truth of His promises. As he draws us into his account of wrestling with the problem, he begins where he ended and where he wants us to settle – the premise and conclusion that God is truly good to His believing people, whatever they may see, or think they see, as they drift into the way of doubting Him. He begins by telling us what God is really like, and goes on to identify those to whom God is and does good. Answers to these questions have been sought along many different lines, not least by biblical saints trying to understand doubts of their own.

Job focused upon God's *omniscience*: "Since times are not hidden from the Almighty, why do those who know Him see not their days?" (Job 24:1). God knows absolutely everything, but He does not enlighten all our darkness. Why not? Surely, He will not leave us in the dark?

Jeremiah looked to God's *justice*: "Righteous are You, O LORD, when I plead with You; Yet let me talk with You about Your judgments. Why does the way of the wicked prosper? Why are those happy who deal so treacherously?" (Jer. 12:1). (That whole chapter speaks to this and will repay serious meditation upon it). Surely He should vindicate the people He loves and saves?

Habakkuk appeals to God's *holiness*: "You are of purer eyes than to behold evil, and cannot look on wickedness. Why do You look on those who deal treacherously, and hold Your tongue when the wicked devours a person more righteous than he?" (Hab. 1:13). Surely a good God would at least intervene against wickedness that oppresses and persecutes the righteous?

Asaph begins by affirming the *goodness* of God, and develops this along three lines:

1. ***God is good***: "Truly God is good to Israel." (73:1a). This is no academic discussion. All these men go to the heart of God's character in one way or another, and each do so in terms of the intimacy of his personal relationship with the Lord. It is, as John Calvin puts it, "as if he had escaped from hell [and] proclaims with a loud voice, and with impassioned feeling, that he had gained a victory." Whatever is painful and distressing in the observed and experienced circumstances, the irreducible truth is that ***God Is Good!***

2. ***God is the Covenant God.*** Notice that the psalmist confesses that God is good "to Israel." (73:1a). This anticipates our next question – as to whom God is good – but it is primarily about who God is. It is the theological and relational bridge between God and His people. He is the covenant God, who promises to save a people from their sins and binds Himself in covenant to do so. "Israel" is not merely a people group in the Middle East – a biological family or ethnicity, who *ipso facto* and exclusively, whatever they do, will experience the goodness of God. To be sure, Israel is – in distinction from the nations, the Gentiles (*goyyim*) all around them – a covenant people, called out by God to be His people, but they are also the people in whom "all the families of the earth" are to "be blessed" in the unfolding of God's plan of salvation (Gen. 12:3). The God who is good – perfectly and impeccably – is the ***God of the covenant*** with His people, "Israel" in the Old Testament and "the Israel of God" in the New (Gal. 6:16).

3. ***God is good "to such as are pure in heart."*** (73:1b). This is the particular answer to the question: "To whom is God good?" – the general answer having already been given as "Israel." It arises from the specific and very personal distress troubling the psalmist. Surely it reminds us of what Jesus will say in the Sermon on the Mount: "Blessed are the pure in heart, for they shall see God." (Matt. 5:8). The heart of the matter is the matter of the heart: "For he is not a Jew who is one outwardly, nor is circumcision that which is outward in the flesh; but he is a Jew who is one inwardly; and circumcision is that of the heart, in the Spirit, not in the letter; whose praise is not from men but from God." (Rom. 2:28-29). This was always true. Here, and in a myriad of Scripture passages, the emphasis is on knowing and loving the Lord from a changed heart; as those who are saved by grace through faith in

Christ, to newness of life. "Who may ascend into the hill of the LORD? Or who may stand in His holy place? He who has clean hands and a pure heart, Who has not lifted up his soul to an idol, Nor sworn deceitfully." (Psalm 24:3-4).

This is no nominal nod and whimsical wink to God's formal existence and Jesus's admirable and exemplary teaching, morals and self-sacrifice. Here is a heart that has closed with Jesus as Savior and Lord in true repentance and faith, and earnestly embraces the holiness of God in love of Him, His Son and His revealed truth; a heart, mind, soul and strength that is transformed and indwelled by the Holy Spirit, with thinking that is captive to Christ, a conscience void of offense and a fervent commitment to discipleship. Notice in all of this, that we cannot but have a growing abundance of reasons to love the Lord. You will see this as Asaph reviews his doubts and affirms afresh the faith he seemed to be losing. And the bedrock of this is in the words, "Truly God is…" and is "good to Israel" – His believing people. God loves His people and His true people love Him, heart, soul and mind (Matt. 22:37).

Asaph, of course is talking about the living God – the God of the Bible – the self-revealed God, without whose revelation, general and special, we would know nothing at all – "the God and Father of our Lord Jesus Christ," through whom alone we can have "redemption through his blood, the forgiveness of sins, according to the riches of his grace." (1 Pet. 1:3; Eph. 1:7). Without this God – Father, Son and Holy Spirit – you are on your own. That's your choice, but if it is, you will discover that "truly" your fictional "god" will have done you *no* "good," and will not save you in time or eternity. Billions of people have their own "God." But these gods are all "dumb idols" of one kind or another (Hab. 2:18) –not excluding the self-deification of the agnostics and atheists of our time. Why? The old Scottish Psalter puts it: [3]

> For all the gods are idols dumb,
> which blinded nations fear;
> But our God is the Lord, by whom
> the heav'ns created were.

---

[3] The 1650 *Scottish Psalter*, Psalm 96, stanza 5.

How Close I Came…

But as for me, my feet had almost stumbled;
My steps had nearly slipped. (Psalm 73:2)

The glory of the Psalms is that they touch our real experience, face real issues honestly, and always lead us to the real Redeemer of God's elect (*cf.* Rom. 8:33). There is nothing of the triumphalism that has become so common in 20th and 21st century churches, with choruses that declare that once you believe in Jesus, you will be saying, "now I am happy all the day,"[4] or, for example, teach us the likes of the unbiblical assertion that we don't need the preaching of God's Law to proclaim and believe the Gospel of Christ, and the impossible notion that the "fear" of the Lord in Scripture is really just a synonym for "love."[5] Apparently, Christians are to be "happy all the day," and untroubled by things like the demands of God's Law and any fears of displeasing Him. Now, of course there is joy all over the Scriptures and certainly in the Psalms. But invariably, joy and peace in

---

[4] The hymn, *Alas and Did My Saviour Bleed*, by Isaac Watts (1674-1748), was augmented – some even think improved (!?) – a century and a half later by a chorus by Ralph Hudson (1843-1901), which ends in the misleading banality which we have quoted: "At the cross, at the cross, where I first saw the light; And the burden of my heart rolled away; It was there by faith I received my sight, And now I am happy all the day!"

[5] Michael Reeves, *Rejoice & Tremble* (Wheaton: Crossway, 2021) pp. 16, 53. On this fear-love relationship, it seems clear enough that treating these words as virtual synonyms, involves violating their obvious and irreducible meaning, thereby obscuring the contrast between them and their importance in, and impact upon, Christian experience. Thus, to say that "perfect love casts out fear" (see 1 John 4:17-18) can only have *meaning and force*, if "fear" is truly fear, with the distinct purpose of representing and exposing a serious problem requiring repentance and renewal, and "love" is truly love, with its distinct purpose of a sanctifying work of the Spirit in renewing that prior lack of faith in exercise. It is surely obvious from Scripture that fear and love are, in their plain and distinctive import, permanently in play in God's dealings with us, in our experience with faith, obedience and indwelling sin.

Furthermore, to interpret this "fear" as just another word for "love," – and even to define it as no more than "reverence" (which is closer to love than fear) – is to diminish and even deny the obvious and ever-present tensions in life (Christians, and also unbelievers) with respect to sin and the righteousness of a holy God – and also with respect to the proper response to the Gospel (in both the converted and the unconverted). The fear=love idea says in effect that, in a true believer, the *fear* of God is merely a psychological weakness, rather than an appropriate and intelligible response to conviction of sin before – and, even more significantly – *from* the Lord's convicting work in the soul. There is love and grace in the terrors of God for all who will have hearing ears and turn to Him afresh. The force of these objective terrors (the fear of God) is necessary in Christian experience (and that of the unconverted) if the real love that casts out the real fear is to become in Christ the fruition of Gospel grace in the sinner's soul and life.

believing frequently follow crises of pain and sorrow – some the impositions of adverse circumstances and the oppressive wickedness of others, but most arising from our own struggles with indwelling sin. In our Savior, we have precious promises and in Him we will be lifted up, as the experiences of His perfect love will overthrow those of warranted fear (1 John 4:18). "Sing praise to the LORD, You saints of His, and give thanks at the remembrance of His holy name. For His anger is but for a moment, His favor is for life; Weeping may endure for a night, but joy comes in the morning." (Psalm 30:4 NKJV).

Asaph is open about his wrestlings with doubt. He neither hides nor denies his temptation to unbelief. W. S. Plumer notes that he "expresses extreme sadness and dejection," and adds that "the cause of this dreadful depression was that he was tempted to give up first truths of religion."[6] This is the real experience of a believer! Asaph confesses "But as for me, my feet had almost stumbled; My steps had nearly slipped." (73:2).

What does he mean by that? Just this – as Matthew Henry puts it – that "the faith even of a strong believer may sometimes be sorely shaken and ready to fail them."[7] Have you never been shaken? Do you believe that as a Christian, what happened to Job, for instance, should never happen to you? Many Christians have been taught that if they do all the right things, everything will go swimmingly in their lives. That's "Home on the Range" theology – "where seldom is heard a discouragin' word, and the skies are not cloudy all day." Don't count on it. When Jesus was "poured out like water" as He suffered for (others') sin, that was one of the most terrible of many moments when He was "in all points tempted," albeit, "without sin." (Psalm 22:14; Heb. 4:15).

This ought to be an encouragement to us – especially in the midst of temptations, pains, doubts and personal failure – not to wallow in these trials, but rather to believe that, "No temptation has overtaken you except such as is common to man," and that "God is faithful, who will not allow you to be tempted beyond what you are able, but with the temptation will also make the way of escape, that you may be able to bear it." (1 Cor. 10:13). Real Christians have real battles, in heart, soul and mind, from all sorts of causes – and not infrequently. It is not a sin to be tempted, but it is a sin to

---

[6] W. S. Plumer D.D., LLD, *Studies in the Book of Psalms* (Edinburgh: Banner of Truth, 1975 [1867]), p. 709.

[7] M. Henry, Vol. 3: 511.

fall. You cannot stop a bird flying over your head, but you don't have to let it build a nest in your hair! Look to the Psalms and lift up your heart to the Lord: and with God's people, cry to the Lord in your trouble and He will save you out of your distresses. (Psalm 107:13).

Why I Almost Slipped ...
(Psalm 73:3-14)

For weal or woe, we tend to compare ourselves to others too much and often with injurious prejudice. Class reunions in TV sitcoms are invariably built around the comedic contrasting of the setbacks and successes of people who haven't crossed paths since they were teens. The real thing, though, is no joke. The psalmist realized he was edging towards a slippery slope upon which mistaken assessments – of others and himself – were leading him towards serious back-sliding that in the end could result in the full-blown apostasy of denying his faith and his God! Having affirmed that he was standing fast in the truth, and established that he no longer continued in the distresses and doubts that he had entertained, Asaph opens up for us the danger, the details and the direction of what is a perennial threat to the lives of even the most committed believers. He identifies the *snare* of envy (v. 3); the *siren-call* of circumstances (vv. 4-12); and the trap of *self-pity* (vv. 13-14). All this, you will notice, is very modern and vitally applicable to all of us today.

The Snare of Envy

"For I was envious of the boastful, When I saw the prosperity of the wicked." (73:3). Asaph *saw* their prosperity and was *envious*. The progression is from seeing to envying. Someone once said that the best way to improve someone's eyesight is not glasses or contact lenses, but a glimpse of other people's success and wealth. Seeing stirs up wanting, and envy makes the goodies look bigger and better than they really are. "Keeping up with Joneses" is a wonderful excuse for conspicuous consumption and shameless stealing. And isn't Madison Avenue largely about the management and manipulation of the economics of envy?

The Siren-call of Circumstances (73:4-12).

Asaph looks even more at the lives of the wicked and it does not do him any good. He inevitably compares what he sees with his own immediate circumstances. He was window-shopping wickedness and the longer he lingered, the more attractive the lives of unbelievers appeared to him to be. We need not tease out all the details of his disaffection from God and His providence: we have all thought about these things at some time or other, and can only too painfully share the psalmist's unhappiness right now. Asaph identifies three main categories in which he saw apparent advantages of unbelief that challenged his faith in the goodness of God. For all their sins, they have:

1. **Liberty to live well**: "For there are no pangs in their death, but their strength is firm. They are not in trouble as other men, nor are they plagued like other men." (73:4-5). Health is indeed a blessing, but are God's people warranted to charge God with over-kindness to those who deny Him?
2. **Freedom to be Me**: "Therefore pride serves as their necklace; Violence covers them like a garment. Their eyes bulge with abundance; They have more than heart could wish. They scoff and speak wickedly concerning oppression; They speak loftily. They set their mouth against the heavens, and their tongue walks through the earth." (73:6-9). This covers self-indulgence, *contra* God's Law and biblical morality, from naked individualism to the fashionable mores of "the herd of independent minds" in any given time. They may be morally debased, but they seem to get off scot-free.
3. **Autonomy from God**: "Therefore his people return here, and waters of a full cup are drained by them. And they say, 'How does God know? And is there knowledge in the Most High?'" (73:10-11). They are their own god, and are accepted, followed and trendy in their contempt for God. And this is just within the Church of the day – never mind the outside world of false religion and (allegedly) no religion!

Asaph summarizes: "Behold, these are the ungodly, who are always at ease; They increase in riches." (73:12). And that, of course, is an abiding standard of "success" in the fallen world of the sons of Adam, who are not converted to Christ and so have not received, in Him, "the adoption as sons" (Gal. 4:5). This pattern is repeated throughout human history and Christian experience: Herod in his palace v. John the Baptizer in his dungeon; Barabbas liberated v. Jesus crucified; and so on *ad infinitum*. There is a parallel here with Job's struggles with the sad setbacks that destroyed his blessedly comfortable life:

Why do the wicked live and become old, Yes, become mighty in power? Their descendants are established with them in their sight, And their offspring before their eyes. Their houses are safe from fear, Neither is the rod of God upon them. Their bull breeds without failure; Their cow calves without miscarriage. They send forth their little ones like a flock, And their children dance. They sing to the tambourine and harp, And rejoice to the sound of the flute. They spend their days in wealth, And in a moment go down to the grave. Yet they say to God, 'Depart from us, For we do not desire the knowledge of Your ways. Who is the Almighty, that we should serve Him? And what profit do we have if we pray to Him?' (Job 21:7-15).

There is a similar complaint from the Prophet Habakkuk in a time of the back-sliding of God's erstwhile people:

You are of purer eyes than to behold evil, and cannot look on wickedness. Why do You look on those who deal treacherously, and hold Your tongue when the wicked devours a person more righteous than he? (Hab. 1:13).

There may well be many times in the life of a child of God when unhappy circumstances lead to the complaint that the Lord has delivered a bad deal. Sometimes it may be only too easy to tell yourself that you might be better off wicked. Remember Jesus's words to His disciples as they face future troubles in their lives and ministries: "These things I have spoken to you, that in Me you may have peace. In the world you will have tribulation; but be of good cheer, I have overcome the world." (Jn. 16:33).

The Self-pity of the "Poor me" mind-set

Asaph allowed himself to wallow in what today we call the "victim-mentality." He said to himself: "Surely I have cleansed my heart in vain, and washed my hands in innocence. For all day long I have been plagued, and chastened every morning." (73:13-14). He indulged regrets for his former commitment to cleansing heart and hands in conformity to the Lord. He now wonders if all he gets in this faith he has professed is being plagued and punished every morning. Poor him!

Why this attitude? The answer is that he was looking at things outwardly, and neither seeing God's revealed will respecting life in this world, nor rightly embracing God's purpose of grace in his life. Does this perhaps give pause to you? Asaph is a serious believer. His experience here, however, ought to be both a humbling and an encouragement to us all. We are never as strong as we think we are, and we tend to depend upon the Lord's enabling grace less than He desires us to. We shall see far more on these things as we continue through the testimony of the psalmist. Suffice it to say at this juncture, that God does all things well, even if His ways are not our ways as to our liking (Mark 7:37; Isa. 55:8-9).

Remember Where Asaph Started and Intends us All to Finish
Truly, God is good... (Psalm 73:1a).

John Hooper was an English preacher and the Anglican Bishop of Gloucester and Worcester who suffered under the Marian persecutions in the 16th century. He could have fled abroad, but said, "I am thoroughly persuaded to tarry, and live and die with my sheep." He was burned at the stake on February 9, 1555. His suffering was awful. He was 45 minutes dying, because of the materials used to kill him. From that stake, his last words were from Psalm 31:5, "Into thine hands I commend my spirit; Thou hast redeemed me, O Lord God of truth." Here is what he had sometime before written on Psalm 73:1:

> All men and women have this life and this world appointed unto them for their winter and season of storms. The summer draweth near, and then shall we be fresh, orient, sweet, amiable, pleasant, acceptable, immortal, and blessed, for ever and ever; and no man shall take us from it. We must, therefore, in the meantime learn out of this verse to sing unto God, whether it be winter or summer, pleasure or pain, liberty or imprisonment, life or death, 'Truly God is loving unto Israel, even unto such as be of a clean heart.'

When we know Christ as our Savior and Lord, will we not understand God's goodness to us – and why the world is the way it is? And in His light, we will see light (Psalm 36:9) – also about ourselves. Asaph began to look away from the Lord and doubt Him. His steps nearly slipped. Perhaps you have felt your feet slipping for similar reasons as his. If so, look to Jesus and glory in the Cross of God's goodness and He will keep your "feet from falling, that [you] may walk before God in the light of life." (Psalm 56:13 ESV).

———————

PART TWO

DISTRESS AND DEVASTATION

Psalm 73:15-21

Chapter 2

Think It Through

If I had said, "I will speak thus," Behold, I would have been untrue to the generation of Your children. ¹⁶ When I thought how to understand this, It was too painful for me— ¹⁷ Until I went into the sanctuary of God; Then I understood their end.
(Psalm 73:15-17)

Asaph tells us in verses 1-14 how he began to doubt God and how as a consequence, his feet had "nearly slipped." (73:2). He saw the prosperity of the godless as contrasted with his less prosperous life, and was tempted to doubt God. He asked himself: "Is God really good?" and "Does He care for me?" He wondered ... and toyed with giving up on the Lord and denying his faith. We know, however, that Asaph was a true believer in the Lord. He affirms this in verse 1. In fact, he was resisting his doubts, fighting his dark thoughts and looking to arrest his fearful slide into a kind of agnostic unbelief.

But how to stop the slide? How to make a stand? How was he to get his heart, soul and mind onto a solid footing again? This is the story of the rest of Psalm 73 (verses 15*ff*). Presently we will focus upon verses 15-17 – which recount the first phase in Asaph's spiritual recovery. He identifies four steps by which his feet are kept from slipping further and something of his former spiritual stability is re-established.

Don't Even Say It!
If I had said, 'I will speak thus,'... (Psalm 73:15a)

Biting your tongue is a first vital step in avoiding entanglement with hasty and potentially dangerous commitments. Asaph did not say what was whirling around in his thoughts. He stopped short of declaring his doubts. Instead, he did what Agur would later advise in Proverbs 30:32, "*If you have been foolish in exalting yourself; Or if you have devised evil, put your hand on your mouth."* This in a general way, in effect codified the example of Job, when he responded to God's gentle challenge of his temerity in correcting and rebuking Him: *"Behold, I am vile; What shall I answer You? I lay my hand over my mouth."* (Job 40:4). Asaph was blessedly silenced *before* he voiced *lèse-majesté* against the King of Glory. Now, why was this so important as a first step in Asaph's restoration to fellowship with the Lord?

The answer is that there is a vital principle here. The Apostle James enjoins us, *"...let every man be swift to hear, slow to speak, slow to wrath; for the wrath of man does not produce the righteousness of God."* (Jas. 1:19-20). You see,

1. You can't listen when you're talking.
2. You can't think when you are pouring out impassioned frustration.
3. You can't learn from God when you're telling Him His faults.
4. You can't grow in grace when you're wallowing in unbelief.
5. You must "be still" if you are to "know that He is God" (Psalm 46:10).

Thinking unworthy thoughts is bad enough. To speak them is to confirm them, to commit yourself to them, and to invite others to agree with you. It is to cross the line from inward doubt to outward rebellion, from private back-sliding to public insurrection, to nail your colors to the mast, and to witness to whatever evil you are propounding. You are actually engaging in the work of the devil, however small the matter may seem to be to you. Putting your hand on your mouth leaves room for reflections rethinking, repentance and renewal. Keep your own counsel, so that you can seek God's counsel!

On Second Thoughts!

Behold, I would have been untrue to the generation of Your children (Psalm 73:15b).

Some count to ten before blurting out their first thoughts. Silent time gives opportunity for another look. Asaph's lesson is: "Always take another look." Take time. Think again. Matthew Henry's advice is simple, "Second thoughts may correct the mistakes of the first."[8] Is that not "common sense"?

---

[8] M. Henry, Vol. 3:513.

Asaph's "Second Thought"

What second thought stopped Asaph's feet from slipping? The answer is: thinking through the consequences for God's children. Where we might have taken our readers through the pros and cons of the existence of God, or the logic or illogic of dealing with adverse providences, Asaph asked himself what would happen to others if he fell away from the faith. He realized in a merciful moment of light that he would be betraying God's people. He would cause them to stumble (*cf*, Matt. 18:6)! He would effectively reject their fellowship and love, which is to say he would break fellowship with them, cease to love them, and thus inevitably do them horrible disservice. David Dickson (1583-1683), the eminent Scottish pastor and theologian of the Second Reformation, observes: "Whosoever condemneth piety and holy conversation, because the world doth so, or because trouble followeth such a course, he doth a high injury to all the saints from the beginning of the world, and to God the author of all holiness ..."[9]

A Very Practical Challenge

The challenge here for we who profess to be the servants of God – not least in our wrestlings with revealed truth and practical faith and practice – is that we stop and ask ourselves if God's children are not precious to us. Consistent faithfulness in an older believer cannot but be an encouragement to the young believer, whereas the vagrant spirituality of doubters and deniers of the Lord can only bring deep discouragement to the family of God. Why? Because, instead of laboring for their encouragement and growth in their faith, we have become effectively crusaders of confusion and missionaries of misery. Questions, however cleverly or even decorously phrased, are not answers. Asaph, by God's grace, understood that sharing his doubts before he had the right answers could only sow seeds of doubts in young hearts, which might cast dark shadows over their souls, in time and perhaps in eternity. Note also, that while no one but a fool will look up to a teacher of Israel who descends into the back-sliding ways of practical unbelief, far less will anyone profit from a shallow, inconsistent and immature professor of faith in Christ. Whose faith will you follow, if, in "considering the end of their conversation," you see only the shipwreck of faith? (Heb. 13:7).

---

[9] D. Dickson, *Psalms* (London: Banner of Truth, 1965 [1653]), Vol. I:451.

A Strategy for Spiritual Crises?

It does not take much of a slip to precipitate a fall. A tiny wet spot on the kitchen floor can easily upset your balance and do serious damage on the way down! Spiritual slippage tends to be a little less sudden and more along the lines of nagging notions and recurrent reservations. Has this touched your life? If so, how should you best respond? The first step – thinking twice, or more – can involve at least three things:

1. Keep to what is *certain*. Only a solid grasp on some *absolute* truth of God's revealed and known will can keep your feet from sliding further. The most bed-rock truth is, of course, that God is good – in Himself and toward His people. That, however, was to be Asaph's conclusion – as, indeed, is stated in 73:1. His starting point, and that of all complainers against, and doubters of, God, is the idea that God is *not* good! It really does not matter which absolute you cling to at first – for Asaph it was betraying God's people. Martyn Lloyd-Jones remarks that standing on the bottom rung of the ladder is better than not being on any rung at all![10]

2. Keep your doubts to *yourself* and *keep thinking*, again and again and again. Too many people seem to think questions are an end in themselves, when in fact they are all journey and no destination. Without some questions you can, to be sure, go nowhere. But to whirl around in a vortex of incessant complaining – and intentionally unresolvable – doubts can only spiral downwards to confusion worse confounded.

3. Keep reflecting on the *consequences* of your doubts and potential answers. What will happen if I continue on this path? Will it be helpful or injurious ... to God's people (love for the brethren); ... to God's cause (love for the Lord); ... and to your soul, your life and your eternal destiny (proper love for yourself)?

For everyone under heaven, whatever their spiritual state and relationship to God, it is about Jesus Christ, and knowing Him as Savior and Lord. O, that you, we all, may be able to say from the heart, by grace though faith: "The LORD is my rock, and my fortress, and my deliverer; my God, my strength, in whom I will trust; my buckler, and the horn of my salvation, and my high tower." (Psalm 18:2).

---

[10] M. Lloyd-Jones, *Faith on Trial* (London: Inter-Varsity Fellowship, 1965), p. 24.

Hang in There!

*When I thought how to understand this,
It was too painful for me— (Psalm 73:16).*

The psalmist "thought" to seek understanding of his problem (73:16a). Is it too obvious to say that not thinking, and not caring to understand, is never a solution? Again and again, you will hear people saying they "just know" something, for which in fact they have not the slightest evidence, nor apparent willingness to face any examination of their assertion. When the well-known star of the TV show, "Cheers," Kirstie Alley, died in December 2022, another famous star declared that he knew they would meet again one day. Easily said: but how, when, where and … whence? Warm sentiments are powerful, but are frequently presumptuous and sometimes without any substance. There is a premium on solid thinking, if solid answers are really desired.

The more Asaph thought, however, the more "painful" the process became for him: it was, he said, "too painful for me." (73:16b). Here is precisely why and where we stop thinking, start sentimentalizing, and go on to seek some means of soul-sedation. The pain of what appears to defy rational resolution soon looks like a reason for giving up and diving into the hopeless anesthesia of distracting diversions in which to drown these sorrows – for example, with the likes of drugs and alcohol. *In extremis*, some will take their own lives. Asaph did not just have a little debate with himself that, in the lazy counsel of ignorant well-wishers, might be dismissed with a glib word like, "Don't worry, it all work out in the end." Thinking through serious issues is often extremely difficult and often forbidding. Some compassion and humble fellow-feeling is in order.

For one thing, *all* thinking involves pain. There is no such thing as a "fun run" if you are to be a seriously competitive athlete. The joy of finishing the race is after the pain of running the race. Every mother knows that the delight of bringing a child into the world is the fruit of birth pangs that may have seemed too painful for her at the time. Thinking – as distinct from dreaming and fantasizing – is real work and can be painful even at the best of times. Escapism and "denial" may seem easy – perhaps even necessary – ways out, but, alas, they can lead nowhere good.

The way the psalmist remembers the pain of his ponderings surely implies that, at the time, he was *not* going to give up. But it also implies that he could see that he was not going to resolve his conundrums by his own unaided thinking and intelligence. He recognized that was beyond him: as Matthew Henry in his Commentary puts words in Asaph's mouth: "I could not conquer it by the strength of my own reasoning."[11] Now, this did not mean that Asaph stopped thinking, still less that he fled into a haze of vapid sentimentalism, but he did come to an end of himself. He "hung in there," as we might say, and continued to grapple with the problem. But he reached out of himself to the Lord, whom he was in some measure trying to deny, and was enabled to persevere in his admittedly embattled faith.

The believers' calling is to persevere determinedly in the faith once delivered to the saints (Jude 3). To do so, we too will need resources beyond and outside of ourselves and man's best efforts, in order that we, in similar trying of our faith, may be preserved from sliding into the abyss of despair, lostness and unbelief.

Seek the Lord!
"Until I went into the sanctuary of God; Then I understood their end." (Psalm 73:17).

All pain was unrelieved, and all doubt still unresolved, says Asaph, until he "went in to the sanctuary of God." The obvious question is: Why did going into the house of God make all the difference, so as to give him understanding and lift the pain that had been troubling him so much?

The Sanctuary of God (73:17a)

The "sanctuary" in this context is the Temple in Jerusalem, so called because it is *God's* Sanctuary – the one place in the world, where, after His people were established in the Promised Land, God manifested His presence, physically and visibly. Here, the Living God commanded and accepted faithful worship and sacrifice for sin, was uniquely present with His covenanted people and there revealed Himself and His will to them through His servants, both priests and prophets. He did so in the *worship* and the feasts in which He was praised and celebrated in the stated Feasts; in the *prayers* in which He nurtured the communion of His people with Himself; and in the truth which informed the heart, mind, soul, and strength of His people through the ministry of the Word.

---

[11] M. Henry, Vol. 3:513.

God does not so presence Himself in the "church" buildings of the New Testament era. Even though the Lord is pleased to draw near to His believing people wherever two or three are gathered together in His name (Matt. 18:20), none of those locations or associated structures should be termed "sanctuaries," or be regarded as "holy places." God's people are, individually and corporately, temples of God (1 Cor. 3:16; 6:19), and Jesus is the way, the truth, and the life for all His people, wherever they are, and no one comes to the Father except through Him (John 14:6).

Nevertheless, in the New Testament era, it is the Christ-instituted Church, where the means of grace are ministered – Word, Sacraments and Prayer – and the weekly worship of the Lord is commanded. It is surely significant for us in our day, that Asaph only came to both understand and resolve his trouble when he "went into" the sanctuary of God. This was not merely "going to church," as that so meagerly represents the commitment of too many today. But Asaph did go physically and spiritually ("into") the unique sanctuary of God's presence in the Old Testament dispensation, certainly in the spirit of David's confession in Psalm 26:8, "LORD, I have loved the habitation of Your house, And the place where Your glory dwells." He went under the glory of the Lord's presence, the ministry of His Word by His sent messengers, and he was instructed and refreshed in his heart soul and spirit. If you are troubled in any way, you cannot expect blessing if you will not worship the Lord with His people, sit under the preaching of the whole counsel of God by His faithful ministers, and hear what God the Lord will say.

Understanding Ultimate Issues (73:17b)

What was it about the "sanctuary" that was used by the Lord to bring Asaph to a sound understanding of his complaint and distress? And why, particularly, was it the understanding of "their end" – the end and destiny of those who do not know the Lord and do not care to know Him to their last breath? What happens in the "sanctuary of God" that sheds light on the lives and "end" of lost people (who will not hear so that their souls may live, Isa. 55:3)? The offering of *sacrifices* surely shed light for Asaph. The Old Testament sacrifices point in two directions: one is to death, and the other is to new life.

1. ***The Reality of Sin***
   The very institution of the OT sacrifices rests upon the fundamental truth – and general principle – that, "The soul who sins shall die."

(Ezek. 18:20), and that this includes the undying death of a lost eternity (Psalm 9:17). The condition and practice of sin against the holy God is punishable by death, in both time and eternity! This is what it means, in biblical/theological terms, to be a child of Adam – to be a fallen human being in a fallen Creation. Sin against the infinite God has infinite implications. God has zero-tolerance for sin, because He *is* perfect righteousness and therefore will not wink at sin, as we self-justifying sinners so easily do in our quest to persuade Him that we are not as bad as all that! (Hab. 1:13).

Here is the basic reality of the human nature we share with our first parents – we are both "in sin ... conceived," and "brought forth in iniquity" (Psalm 51:5). And "There is none righteous, no not one..." (see Rom. 3:10-18); and so our "carnal" minds are "enmity against God" (Rom. 8:7). There is no escaping this basic condition of the "natural" man. He will not, does not, and by nature cannot "receive the things of the Spirit of God, for they are foolishness to him; nor can he know them, because they are spiritually discerned." (1 Cor. 2:14). Disagree all you want, Christian, but all that will prove is the truth of God's revealed Word about the true state of sinners, and the fact that you don't know your Bible!

The immediate implication and application that bears upon Asaph's problem concerns the importance he gives, in his doubting of God, to the importance for his life of material circumstances – namely, his relative poverty as a servant of God *versus* the prosperity of people who couldn't care less about the things of God! It is as if Asaph has become convinced that the most important thing about human life is "doing well." And since he wasn't doing well, but the openly wicked were, he was losing out even to the extent that God was the failure that was making his life less than his life should be. Jesus gives us the corrective to this thoroughly superficial – and perniciously dangerous – understanding of what is really important in life: "Take heed and beware of covetousness, for one's life does not consist in the abundance of the things he possesses." (Luke 12:15). That clearly applies to more than money and stuff. Jesus has a word in the Sermon on the Mount that must surely come as a rude shock to the religious godless, and the unconverted church-goers of our day:

"Not everyone who says to Me, 'Lord, Lord,' shall enter the kingdom of heaven, but he who does the will of My Father in heaven.

Many will say to Me in that day, 'Lord, Lord, have we not prophesied in Your name, cast out demons in Your name, and done many wonders in Your name?' And then I will declare to them, 'I never knew you; depart from Me, you who practice lawlessness!'" (Matt. 7:21-23).

Sin and death put the happiness of the godless and the worldliness of the professing Christians in proper perspective. Solomon's injunction is of universal application to believers and unbelievers alike: "There is a way that seems right to a man, but its end is the way of death." (Prov. 14:12). Jesus says: "If you love me, you will keep my commandments." (John 14:15 ESV).[12] OK... Do you?

2. **The Provision of Salvation**

    The institution of the OT sacrifices also presupposes the provision of salvation from sin and death. What were the annual sacrifices, the furniture in the Temple and, in spite of sin in God's people, the presence of the Shekinah glory all about? And what light is there here for Asaph – and the rest of us? There is a double answer to this...

    You need a Savior!

    And however successful, healthy and long-lived you may be, you had better know this Savior, because these other things can never save you and take you to heaven. So, Jesus says: "Do not lay up for yourselves treasures on earth, where moth and rust destroy and where thieves break in and steal; but lay up for yourselves treasures in heaven, where neither moth nor rust destroys and where thieves do not break in and steal. For where your treasure is, there your heart will be also." (Matt. 6:19-21). And why did Jesus tell Nicodemus, "You must be born again." (John 3:7)?

    There is a Savior!

    Asaph, you are on the way to denying Him, when you need Him all the more! But you are a believer, so be what you are already in your Redeemer God and return to Him. And that is what happened to Asaph, under the influence of the Spirit of God, who awakened his conscience to God's gracious provision of a plan of salvation for

---

[12] ESV is to be preferred, since, while the first part of the verse is present tense, the latter part is a future indicative ("you will keep"). Jesus is setting out the dynamic of genuine discipleship and laying it upon the consciences of His hearers and readers – including you and me!

sinners like him. This is a word to all who profess Christ as their Savior and regard themselves as believers. Are you a real believer in Jesus as your Savior? Then be what you are *in Him*! This is, of course, of wider application than that revealed to the doubting believers like Asaph. It is a call to the lost and unbelieving to flee the wrath to come, and, in repentance and faith, to trust in Him as your Savior and Lord, personally and from the heart.

The Savior promised throughout the Psalms is Jesus Christ, Son of God and son of man. What do we need and what can He give? Every "natural man" needs a new nature, a new heart, a new record, and a new life. In contrast to that, all the prosperity of the godless does *absolutely nothing good* for their salvation. But Jesus Christ gave Himself on Calvary's cross as the Substitute for sinners like you and me. He died for the ungodly, precisely to regenerate dead souls, forgive the unforgivable, give new life to empty and doomed lives, and bring the hell-bent to heaven. Is it time for you too to think again about your relationship to the Lord, and will you, like Asaph of old, go into the house of God, that you might understand your own end – and call upon the Lord that you might be saved? (Acts 2:21). Remember Jesus's solemn words of gracious invitation: "I tell you, ... unless you repent you will all likewise perish. (Luke 13:3, 5). The promise of the Gospel stands as you read these words from God: "For God so loved the world that He gave His only begotten Son, that whoever believes in Him should not perish but have everlasting life." (John 3:16); and, "Whoever calls on the name of the LORD shall be saved." (Acts 2:21; quoting Joel 2:32).

Chapter 3

Grasping The Real Issue

Surely You set them in slippery places; You cast them down to destruction. [19] Oh, how they are brought to desolation, as in a moment! They are utterly consumed with terrors. [20] As a dream when one awakes, So, Lord, when You awake, You shall despise their image. (Psalm 73:18-20)

When Asaph looked at the world around him, he saw godless people prospering (73:3-12), and he was tempted to think that he was wasting his time committing his life to God (73:13-14). As he confessed, his "steps had nearly slipped" (73:2). He had not yet rejected the faith for full-blown unbelief and apostasy. He had, however, struggled with his doubts and knew that if things continued along this line, he would soon be on a distinctly downward trajectory in terms of his faith and walk with the Lord. Spiritual depression will do this to us, unless something happens to stop the rot and recall us to revived devotion. It is not as if discouragement and spiritual distress are uncommon in the normal lives of Christians in this world. And it ought to surprise no-one that God's Word is full of words addressing such trials in our lives. – most affectingly, in the Psalms of Lament of the Bible's praise book.[13] Asaph authored at least twelve Psalms (50, 73-83), of which three (74, 79 and 80) are Psalms of Lament.

What started to stop the rot for Asaph was his decision to worship in the Temple: "I went into the sanctuary of God." We might just say, "He

---

[13] Psalms of Lament include many that are individually focused, such as Psalms 3, 5-7, 13, 17, 22, 25-28, 32, 38, 39, 42, 43, 51, 54-57, 59, 61, 63, 64, 69-71, 86, 88, 102, 109, 120, 130 and 140-43. There are also some that are communal in their thrust, as Psalms 44, 60, 74, 79, 80, 85, 86, and 90. As the one and only divinely inspired and authorized hymnbook - "Book of Praises" (Hebrew, *Sepher Tehillim*) – the Bible's Psalter consists of a collection of divinely inspired psalms, hymns and songs, which unsurprisingly speaks to the whole range of real life-experience, including the lamentable as well as the joyful – in obvious contrast to the happy weightlessness of so many modern hymn- and chorus-books.

[39]

went to church," but that is way too simplistic and even misleading. There are – as we all know from personal experience – churches and churches. And sometimes, for not a few Christians, there can be no organized solid Christ-proclaiming, Gospel-offering and Bible-expounding churches within reach. There are always, in this world, believers who are meeting, so to speak, "in the catacombs," and some whose only consolation is found in Malachi 3:16: "Then those who feared the LORD spoke to one another, And the LORD listened and heard them; So a book of remembrance was written before Him For those who fear the LORD And who meditate on His name." (Mal. 3:16). The Temple as founded by God was a unique institution, where He "physically" manifested Himself, revealed His will to His people. The order of worship in, the structure of the Temple itself, and even its furniture, breathed the way of salvation for sinners by nature. It foreshadowed the coming of the Lord's Anointed (Messiah), Christ, the Savior. Rightly understood and applied it is archetypical of what the Church and Christians are meant to be – temples of the Holy Spirit (1 Cor. 3:16; 2 Cor. 6:16).

Asaph looked for answers in the right place and apparently with the right spirit. Central to the ministry of "the sanctuary of God," was the necessity of sacrifice for sin, on account of the hell-bent lostness of godless humanity. This contrasts with the many complainers against God in our day, whether they "go to church" or not, who rather ignore the Bible, sound worship, faithful ministry of the "means of grace," and the fellowship of the people of God – exhibiting attitudes that argue something of a reprobate mind, rather than any sincere interest in the Lord or the truth.

What was crucial in Asaph's odyssey was that he went to the source of truth – which was God manifesting Himself in the Temple. And what answers did he find there? He found three things that deeply touched his experience – things he no doubt had been well-acquainted with before his present struggles. Now, by the work of the Spirit of God, Asaph's soul was to be restored again (Psalm 23:3):

1. God's presence with His Word for his predicament.
2. God's provision of sacrifices for his sin: blood sacrifices providing for salvation, in a Savior received by faith.
3. Clarity on the awful end of the lost and the realization he was envying people who were ruining their lives and in danger of hell, unless they were saved from their predicament!

This is how Asaph came to understand that he was going the way of practical unbelief – the broad way that leads to destruction (Matt. 7:13) – and so returned to "the path of life," in which God's "presence is fullness of joy," and at whose "right hand are pleasures forevermore (Psalm 16:11)."

Now, in 73:18-20, we are shown how Asaph's understanding of the real issues – life and death in time and eternity – begins to crystallize and bring him ever closer to a re-affirmation of his faith. He answers two basic questions: 1. Should I envy the success of the godless? (73:18-20a); and, 2. Is God asleep while the godless prosper and the godly suffer? (73:20b).

Envy the success of the wicked?

Remember the issue for the Psalmist. Openly godless folk seemed to be doing fine in life, while he, who was concerned to love God and keep His commandments, seemed only to get a hard life out of his godliness. You can see what had coursed through his mind: why bother with God and faithfulness if the result is trouble? So, he envied successful unbelievers!

This is not to be loftily dismissed as some proof of not being a real believer, as if truly faithful souls would never do such a thing. All our ordinary troubles – how much more the extraordinary ones – are real challenges to our spiritual equilibrium. The prosperity of the wicked – and the hardships of the righteous – pose real questions that deserve and require solid answers. Not without difficulty, Asaph makes four observations about the success of those who care nothing for the living God, and who glory in their accomplishments, whether health, wealth, influence, power or fame. This "success" is, however, not what it seems for these reasons:

1. It is *temporary* success: "Surely You set them in slippery places" (73:18a). All that glistens in their lives is not gold. In reality, God has set them in "slippery places." They, of course, are happy with their attainments and their happy circumstances. They don't see themselves as not really being on solid ground. Plenty people build houses on the sands of pride, presumption and plain foolishness (Matt. 7:26). They seem to get away with it – at least for a while. Like beach houses in the Carolinas and California, they can't last forever.

2. It is *doomed* success: "You cast them down to destruction" (73:18b). This ruin, says Matthew Henry, [14] with characteristic Puritan pithiness, will be…

"… sure and inevitable," – that is, a reckoning will come.
"… swift and sudden," – it will be a surprise to you.
"… severe and very dreadful," – it will be comprehensive in its justice.

Short of repentance toward God and faith in the Lord Jesus Christ, the prosperous ungodly, like all persevering unbelievers, "shall be punished with everlasting destruction from the presence of the Lord and from the glory of His power, when He comes, in that Day, to be glorified in His saints and to be admired among all those who believe, because our testimony among you was believed." (2 Thess. 1:9-10). Such success will come to an inevitable end, if not in time, then in eternity. Therefore, it is a…

3. It is *pitiable* success: "Oh, how they are brought to desolation, as in a moment! They are utterly consumed with terrors." (73:19). Is it not unutterably sad to contemplate the wreckage in time and for eternity of the "successful" who are "without God in the world" and, in reality, have no hope for time and eternity (Eph. 2:12)? Lloyd-Jones is on target when he notes: "There is nothing so hopeless in the world, ultimately, as the bankruptcy of the non-Christian view of life."[15] The same author cites words of Alfred, Lord Tennyson, in his poem of 1833, *In Memoriam*:

> Our little systems have their day;
> They have their day and cease to be:
> They are but broken lights of thee,
> And thou, O Lord, art more than they.

4. It is *illusory* success: "As a dream when one awakes, So, Lord, when You awake, You shall despise their image." (Psalm 73:20). The now retired

---

[14] M. Henry, Vol. 3:514.
[15] Lloyd-Jones, *op. cit.*, 51. Writing 60 years ago, Lloyd-Jones goes on to relate certain the sad observations of Charles Darwin (the pioneer of evolutionism) and H. G. Wells (in his book *Mind at the End of its Terror*), as they record their deep disillusionment at the end of their lives.

tennis star, Andre Agassi (b. 1970), once did a camera advertisement, in which he declared "Image is everything." Whatever he actually thought about that idea, our verse certainly tells what the Lord thinks about it! That kind of "image" – or we might say, "vision" – is no more substantial than a "dream." It is no better than an illusion. Do you recall the "vision" of the rich man in Luke 12:19-21? He said to himself: "'Soul, you have many goods laid up for many years; take your ease; eat, drink, and be merry.' But God said to him, 'Fool! This night your soul will be required of you; then whose will those things be which you have provided?' So is he who lays up treasure for himself, and is not rich toward God." (Lk. 12:19-21).

In Psalm 52, the psalmist contemplates the destruction of the wicked, and the contrast with his own destiny as a true child of God: "'Here is the man who did not make God his strength, but trusted in the abundance of his riches, and strengthened himself in his wickedness.' But I am like a green olive tree in the house of God; I trust in the mercy of God forever and ever. I will praise You forever, because You have done it; and in the presence of Your saints I will wait on Your name, for it is good." (Psalm 52:7-9).

What then, is there to envy in the prosperity and successes of folk who are lost and unbelieving? ...who are without hope (Eph. 2:12)? ...who are without Christ? ...and who don't begin to care about the things of God? Should we not weep for them, rather than wail about our lack of earthly health and wealth? Should we not be crying out to the Lord for their salvation, and glorying in the cross of Christ for ours, received and enjoyed? We have "this treasure in earthen vessels" and are being filled by "the fountain of living waters," whereas they are presently empty vessels that are no better than "broken cisterns, that can hold no water." (2 Cor. 4:7; Jer. 2:13). Compassion – not envy – is the right response of a godly soul!

Is God Asleep?

The words, "So, Lord, when you awake..." (73:20a) might seem to imply that the Lord is asleep while the godless prosper and the godly suffer. We know, of course, that "He who keeps Israel shall neither slumber nor sleep." (Psalm 121:4). God is *never* asleep – but His judgments often are! What awakens at some point is the reckoning. Why this delay? Why does

He allow – no, decree – so much wickedness to go on, apparently unchecked? Why, indeed, is this sin-sick fallen world itself still marching on through history, leaving so much wreckage in its wake? Here are some basic answers:

1. The sinfulness of sin is exposed. The true colors, so to speak, come shining through. Leave a peach on the kitchen counter and it will look great for a while. But watch what the previously invisible world does with it – it isn't a pretty picture! The course of life unveils, in the first instance, the character and consequences of sin. But it further reveals, in the second place, the reality of God's redemptive work in those He saves to be His people. Proverbs 11:5 explains: "The righteousness of the blameless will direct his way aright, but the wicked will fall by his own wickedness." Similarly, Proverbs 24:16 says that "a righteous man may fall seven times and rise again, but the wicked shall fall by calamity."

   The concluding application to the Lord's people is: "Do not fret because of evil-doers, nor be envious of the wicked." (Prov. 24:19). This parallels the thought in Psalm 73:20b: "So, Lord, when You awake, You shall despise their image." The wicked may presently be prospering and may look invincible on account of the seeming permanence, pervasiveness and predominance of godless practice in the affairs of human beings at every level – but when the Lord awakens His judgments in the Great Day, we shall see all that evil "despised" forever under "the wrath of the Lamb" (Rev. 6:16). The Lamb of God who takes away the sin of the world He came to save to Himself (John 1:29, 36), is also the Lion of Judah who judges the world of sinners (Rev. 5:5-6).

2. The long-suffering of God is revealed. Scripture everywhere teaches us that: "The LORD *is* merciful and gracious, Slow to anger, and abounding in mercy." (Psalm 103:8). That is how he planned from the start to save people from every generation in the history of this world He has created. Part of this is His long-suffering, by which He decrees the continuance of fallen mankind in the generations of humanity in His world and even the mixed multitude of "wheat" and "tares" – that is, converted and unconverted – in His visible Church on earth (Matt. 13:25*f*). It is God's grace that requires these situations so that He may

save sinners from every generation and kindred over the millennia before Christ comes again at the consummation of all things. Thus, he says of His people in Nehemiah's day:

"They refused to obey, and they were not mindful of Your wonders that You did among them. But they hardened their necks, and in their rebellion they appointed a leader to return to their bondage. But You are God, ready to pardon, gracious and merciful, slow to anger, abundant in kindness, and did not forsake them." (Neh. 9:17)

This world is not meant to be heaven, nor can it be heaven, but this is exactly what makes it the arena of salvation. It is a place where there are lost people that God is calling to Himself that they may be saved – that place He so loves that He sent His only begotten Son that whoever believes in Him should not perish but have everlasting life. (John 3:16).

3. The love of God for His people is confirmed. When bad things happen to us, the natural tendency is to wonder where God has gone. It is the kind of "natural" that feels robbed of something to which we thought ourselves entitled, or from which we assumed some exemption. It is the kind of "natural" that is thoroughly understandable, but it is the kind of "natural" for which even saved sinners need "the grace of our Lord Jesus Christ, the love of God and the communion of the Holy Spirit." These words of the Corinthian benediction (2 Cor. 13:14) are not a given to us as a cue to pick up our Bibles and go home for Sunday lunch. They are the promise of our Triune God for every minute of the Christian life, whether awake or asleep, and all to the restoring our souls, the reviving of our hearts, the instruction of our thoughts and the animation of our actions. He is the God who is love, and, "In this the love of God was manifested toward us, that God has sent His only begotten Son into the world, that we might live through Him. (1 John 4:9). And "who shall separate us from the love of Christ? Shall tribulation, or distress, or persecution, or famine, or nakedness, or peril, or sword? (Rom. 8:35). Shall we not then exult in the matchless love of our precious Savior?

4. The Lord does "awaken" as promised. In His sovereignty, He puts the happy careless and prospering wicked on slippery places; in His righteousness, He visits sudden and condign punishment upon His

unrepentant enemies; and, in His everlasting love and faithfulness, He preserves His believing people from slipping themselves. As we already saw, this "awakening' is to execute judgment deferred. This does not mean the Lord has been asleep in His care of His people – or indeed is not also dealing with those who are not believers. He who keeps Israel never slumbers nor sleeps (Psalm 121:4). And if He does not heal our diseases, or lift other burdens, as we might wish and pray for – and even expect – we are assured that, meantime, His grace will be sufficient for us (2 Cor. 12:9). And in every event, "the Lord is faithful, who will establish you and guard you from the evil one. (2 The. 3:3).

Understanding

The vital issue that we need to grasp – for time and eternity – concerns our personal relationship to, and with, the Living God. This encompasses understanding His character and His dealings with us, in all the ups and downs of the fallenness of the world and the vagaries of our own character and sinfulness, from the womb to the grave, and from time to eternity. Simply put, we need a Savior – and He has been sent to this needy world to "save His people from their sins." (Matt. 1:21). The immediate occasion of our need of a Savior, as revealed in the Seventy-third Psalm, is a trial of faith in one who is already a believer. Asaph is assailed by doubts that are set to put him upon a slippery slope toward practical unbelief. He was tempted to envy the prosperity of the wicked. He entertained the thought that God had failed him and he wondered if he might be better off being less rigorous in his devotion to the Lord. But he went into the Temple, and was evidently convinced afresh about the nature of the ministry and the truth of God. He stepped back from the brink of denying his faith and his Lord, and began to make application of God's truth to his life, both inward and outward, heart and hand, past, present and future.

There is the most searching – and encouraging – application here to every child of God wrestling with costs of discipleship in the face of hard providences in the external circumstances of a world hostile to both God's revealed will and the faithful witness of His people. Not to be missed, however, is also a word of warning and implicit invitation to all who are strangers to the grace God in the Gospel. Both concern the issue of the need of every sinner in this world for a saving knowledge of the Lord Jesus Christ.

1. To the unbelieving, the message is that *freedom from Jesus Christ*, in everything from simple ignorance of the facts, to indifference to the Word of truth, and on to opposition and complete denial of the claims of God, is a desperate dream doomed to destruction – if not in this life, certainly at the moment passing from it into eternity. The prophet Isaiah says that,

    "It shall even be as when a hungry man dreams, and look – he eats; But he awakes, and his soul is still empty; Or as when a thirsty man dreams, And look – he drinks; But he awakes, and indeed he is faint, and his soul still craves: So the multitude of all the nations shall be, who fight against Mount Zion." (Isa. 29:8).

    This is no mere prophecy of doom, as the too common caricatures of the careless like to laugh off serious warnings. It implicitly calls everybody to flee the wrath to come, in repentance and faith, and be saved. Isaiah later shares Christ's call to all sinners: "Incline your ear, and come to Me. Hear, and your soul shall live; And I will make an everlasting covenant with you – The sure mercies of David." (Isa. 55:3). Jesus says, "He who has ears to hear, let him hear!" (Matt. 13:9).

2. To the believing, the message is that *freedom in Jesus Christ* is the new life you already have from Him, both now and forever. What then is the goal and end of the godly life – that is, believer, your life in Christ, life in your risen Savior, your future in time and eternity? It is not total freedom from all troubles, but it is freedom to share in, and grow from, Jesus' overcoming the world. After warning his followers of troubles to come, Jesus assures them:

    "These things I have spoken to you, that in Me you may have peace. In the world you will have tribulation; but be of good cheer, I have overcome the world." (John 16:33).

    How then shall we live? The answer is: Be what you are in Christ – by His enabling grace. Let it be said of you: "Mark the blameless man, and observe the upright; For the future of that man is peace." (Psalm 37:37). Let it be hoped by you: "The path of the just is like the shining sun, that shines ever brighter unto the perfect day." (Prov. 4:18). And may you testify with the Apostle Paul: "Finally, there is laid up for me the crown of righteousness, which the Lord, the righteous Judge, will give to me on that Day, and not to me only but also to all who have loved His appearing." (2 Tim. 4:8). We are called to a life marked, not only by practical godliness, but also with "peace in believing."

"Now may the God of hope fill you with all joy and peace in believing, that you may abound in hope by the power of the Holy Spirit." (Rom. 15:13).

Chapter 4

Grieving Your Guilt

Thus my heart was grieved, And I was vexed in my mind.
²² I was so foolish and ignorant; I was like a beast before You.
(Psalm 73:21-22)

"Guilty, My Lord!" is undoubtedly the most unpopular plea made before British judges, whether in a real court or in a fictional court-room drama. It is, however, the plea that God wants to hear from every child of Adam. It ought to be a fruit of everyone's reflection on the motives and actions in life. Martyn Lloyd-Jones is surely correct when he says that "there is no possible growth in the Christian life unless we are ruthlessly honest with ourselves."[16] That means facing our weaknesses, faults, desires, personality traits and our habitual and besetting sins. We need to be clear in our heart and mind as to where we really stand with God our Father and Jesus His Son.

Perhaps you have noticed how Asaph came to be willing to examine himself. He saw wicked folk doing fine in life – physically, materially and socially – he doubted it was worth following God's way. He felt that all he got out of it was problems. At that point, he went to the Temple and that helped to straighten out his thinking. He saw...

1. that God was true, good and just;
2. that the prosperity of the wicked was temporary and illusory;
3. that judgment was just around the corner; and
4. that he himself had been foolishly dabbling with practical unbelief, and was in urgent need of the Lord and a closer walk with Him.

---

[16] M. Lloyd-Jones, *op. cit.*, 75.

Self-examination with spiritual discernment is a vital – and perennial – necessity for all of us; and that brings us to the psalmist's awakening to his true spiritual condition.

Accepting Responsibility
*Thus my heart was grieved,
and I was vexed in my mind. (Psalm 73:21).*

Honest self-examination is, as already noted, a vital spiritual exercise in the believer. The apostle enjoined the Corinthians: "Examine yourselves *as to* whether you are in the faith. Test yourselves. Do you not know yourselves, that Jesus Christ is in you? – unless indeed you are disqualified." (2 Cor. 13:5). It is possible to get a formally correct view of God and a sound grasp of the danger facing unbelieving people, and yet not squarely face up to your own true spiritual condition. Why? Because the real issue is having a right relationship with the Lord.

Asaph had been edging toward the attitude, in which he saw himself as the innocent victim wronged, no less, by God. God seemed to him not to care about the hardships facing His hitherto faithful servant, but was ready to allow the godless – His enemies – to enjoy "the good life!" We are used to the "victimization" theme in modern life, in which people complain about other people on all sorts of subjects, serious and trivial – but this is the ultimate victimization story – God's servants as victims of God Himself![17] The first thing God does – in His grace and love for a conflicted believer – is to bring him to take responsibility for what he was thinking in his heart and mind.

The struggling psalmist – in his time in "the sanctuary of God," – was refreshed in his understanding of the true condition of the unconverted. The Lord brings him to the most humbling of convictions: "Thus my heart was grieved, and I was vexed in my mind." (73:21). The text is *reflexive*, its force being that he recognizes that he brought this grief and vexation upon himself. This is important, because so much of our grief and vexation is

---

[17] Arguably, the most extreme accusation of this idea is that of the late atheist, Christopher Hitchens, when he charged that God's punishing Jesus for the sins of others should be viewed as the ultimate case of "child abuse." Hitchens attributed no reality to God, Jesus, the Cross or the atonement in the first place, but was proposing a *reductio ad absurdum* to show what he saw as the warped and impossible logic at the heart of the Christian faith – and thereby adding blasphemy to blasphemy in his war against God.

blamed upon others, sometimes justifiably, to be sure. Here, however, Asaph is reflecting his sorrow and complaints back on himself.

At first, he had blamed everybody else. *God* let the wicked go scot-free, while giving him a hard time. *Other people* were doing better that he, and he was envious of them. But was it their fault that Asaph was envious? Was it God's fault that he questioned God's goodness and fairness? What Asaph observed had a certain truth in it – and still does today. The wicked did – and still do – prosper, and God does not immediately rain fire on them. But does that excuse the people of God being envious, angry, skeptical and unbelieving? Do we really think we are morally superior to God, and know better than He as to how things should be done?[18] Asaph came to recognize his error, took responsibility, and accepted blame for his attitude, and, as we shall see, went on to repent and return to the Lord.

Exercising Repentance
… my heart was grieved (Psalm 73:21)

A heart grieved before and toward the Lord, as Asaph's now is, is beginning to express repentance. He is saying – in classical language – *Mea culpa!* ("I am guilty!"), and *"Peccavi!"* ("I have sinned"), with complete sincerity and surrender. He is confessing that he had given himself to anger, to ill-considered and unbelieving thoughts and feelings – and was all wrong! This is the conviction of sin that you see all over the Scriptures. You will notice that repentance is a lot more than feeling sorry and "moving on." Still less is it a mere form of words. Here are a few examples:

1. Job says to God: "I have heard of You by the hearing of the ear, but now my eye sees You. Therefore I abhor myself, and repent in dust and ashes." (Job 42:5). Abhorring yourself and pondering your past sins in dust and ashes is not popular in modern churches and is often decried as a species of morbid introspection. Repentance does indeed herald a renewal of a sense of God's love for the returning sinner, but cannot

---

[18] This conceit of flawed human thinking is summed up in popular expressions like a beautiful song in the musical, Pickwick, by the eponymous protagonist: "If I ruled the world, every day would be the first day of Spring." Verse after verse, it builds a picture of a secular heaven on earth – a wondrous dream, no doubt, but a fantasy doomed to unrelieved failure. In Dickens' novel, Mr. Pickwick is a well-meaning master of comic disaster – and that is what is represented in the song.

but involve serious and particular reflections on damage done, pain inflicted, sin aggravated and relationships broken – and the future actions in the restored soul and life that are appropriate to rebuilding the ruins wreaked across the spectrum of both the inner life and outward relationships. The idea expressed in the 1970 romantic movie, "Love Story," that "Love means never having to say you're sorry," sounds wonderful, but denies anything remotely like repentance, if not even the notion that doing wrong to someone has any relevance to harmony between the parties involved. Loving the Lord *requires* repentance. Not repenting is a repudiation and denial of the love of the Lord in sending His Son to die for sinners, and is despising Christ in "the death of the Cross." (Phil. 2:8).

2. The prodigal son, in his repentance, says to himself: "I will arise and go to my father, and will say to him, 'Father, I have sinned against heaven and before you, and I am no longer worthy to be called your son.'" (Luke 15:18-19). Sin is always costly, and repentance is costly for the repentant (and too costly for the unrepentant). The father receives the son without a *post mortem* and further penalties (as the brother evidently wished). Our Father in heaven receives truly repentant sinners, both converted unbelievers and returning backsliders; but faith and repentance are of a different order from the standard evangelical rote repetition of a one sentence so-called "sinner's prayer" to "receive Jesus."

3. The Apostle Paul says to the repentant Corinthian Christians: "Now I rejoice, not that you were made sorry, but that your sorrow led to repentance. For you were made sorry in a godly manner, that you might suffer loss from us in nothing. For godly sorrow produces repentance leading to salvation, not to be regretted; but the sorrow of the world produces death. For observe this very thing, that you sorrowed in a godly manner: What diligence it produced in you, what clearing of yourselves, what indignation, what fear, what vehement desire, what zeal, what vindication! In all things you proved yourselves to be clear in this matter." (2 Cor. 7:9-11). Here is concrete evidence of genuine repentance.

Will you apply this to your own heart? Are you grieved over something or somebody? Who is to blame? Is it truly somebody else … or are you shifting the blame to that person? I once met a grieved old lady, who blamed the church of her early life for her never getting married. It was the first thing she told me about herself, and it had clearly dominated her long and apparently lonely life. Are you blaming the church, or other people, for something in your life that could really be your problem? Asaph discovered he had put a dagger in his own soul – and by God's grace he turned in repentance to the Lord for healing.

Keeping Heart and Mind
I was vexed in my mind. (73:21b)

Seeking renewal in heart and mind is now on Asaph's agenda. Every repentant rethink will carry the felt need of applying God's Word, in Jesus Christ and by filling one's thinking on every vexation with God's Word, in Jesus Christ and by the Holy Spirit. The more darkness, the greater the need of light. Our problems invariably involve leaving Christ and God's Word out of the picture. This is true whether the vexations arise from external impositions from adverse circumstances, or from personal and internal trials, including matters of health and faith. Jesus warns us that, in the face of trials and tribulations, "The love of many shall grow cold." (Matt. 24:12). That is the result, of course, of going with the "flesh" rather than the Holy Spirit speaking in the Scriptures.

Listen to the Apostle Paul: "Be anxious for nothing, but in everything by prayer and supplication, with thanksgiving, let your requests be made known to God; and the peace of God, which surpasses all understanding, will guard your hearts and minds through Christ Jesus." (Phil. 4:6).

And Solomon: "Keep your heart with all diligence, for out of it spring the issues of life." (Prov. 4:23). This is followed with practical advice:

1. "Put away from you a deceitful mouth, and put perverse lips far from you." (v. 24).
2. "Let your eyes look straight ahead, and your eyelids look right before you." (v. 25).
3. "Ponder the path of your feet, and let all your ways be established. Do not turn to the right or the left; remove your foot from evil." (vv. 26-27).

The Savior is the Lord Jesus Christ: "Create in me a clean heart, O God, and renew a steadfast spirit within me." (Psalm 51:10), and operative standard for faithfulness is the Word of God: "Your Word is a lamp to my feet and a light to my path." (Psalm 119:115).

PART THREE

DELIVERANCE

Psalm 73:22-28

Chapter 5

Grace

I was so foolish and ignorant; I was like a beast before You.
²³ Nevertheless I am continually with You;
You hold me by my right hand.
(Psalm 73:22-23)

With conviction of sin, Asaph's "before" has begun to transition to his "after." The time when he was tempted to doubt the Lord, and to abandon his commitment to living for Him as a disciple, was a dark experience. The Lord, however, never abandoned him, but used it to lead him to a larger view of His amazing grace.

It is an example for us all of how the Lord will sometimes let us "stew in our own juice" when we have set ourselves to drift away from Him, or deny Him altogether. But He does not abandon His own. It is His grace when he lets us struggle with some of the consequences of our sin and reminds us – we are speaking here of the Lord's dealings with believers who profess faith in Him – that He did not give us "the Spirit of adoption by whom we cry out, 'Abba, Father,'" for us to turn away from Him and "receive the spirit of bondage again." (Rom. 8:15). He rattles that spiritual cage we seem to be edging towards in our back-sliding and reminds us that it is "a fearful thing to fall into the hands of the living God." (Heb. 10:31).

This is unfolded in detail in the second part of the psalm (verses 21-28), which is the applicatory section of Asaph's description of his doubts and deliverance. There are four main themes in these verses:

1. He, as we have seen, confesses sin and repents toward God (v. 21);
2. He acknowledges God's goodness in restoring him (vv. 22-23);
3. He reaffirms his faith in the Lord (vv. 24-26); and
4. He resolves to follow a closer walk with God in the future (vv. 27-28)

In the previous chapter, we looked at Asaph's confession of sin and his nascent repentance (v. 21). We now take up his reflections on his low spiritual state *before* that work of the Lord's grace in his heart (v. 22) and his revived spiritual condition *after* it (v. 23). He testifies to his earlier foolishness, and to his later renewed walk with God, by His free grace. The Lord's invisible hand had kept him from falling away utterly and had graciously delivered him from his doubt, to restore his fellowship with the Lord in renewed understanding, obedience, and the joy of salvation. In this transformation, Asaph sees and acknowledges that God has been good to him all along.

Foolish and Ignorant
I was so foolish and ignorant (Psalm 73:22a).

We rightly tell our children to be careful about calling people foolish or stupid, but we do well to admit our own stupidity before the Lord. God defines "the fool" as the one who says *in his heart*, "there is no God." (Psalm 14:1). This is not limited to professing atheists. It is one way to describe *practical* unbelief, even in a believer.

Asaph declares he was "so foolish," but he was never an atheist. However, he did let his heart and mind go on *as if* there were no God. This is how he became a fool in his backsliding. The reality is that if we will not listen to the Lord, and act as if He does not exist, we will answer for our own foolishness, and will only have ourselves to blame. And if you know your own heart, you know that you have been foolish many times, whether in things so small as to seem trivial, or in large blunders which have chased you down your life.

Asaph also says he was "ignorant." This is not an excuse, as if he really had no idea about what he was doing. This ignorance is what we don't know when we don't *want* to know! Supposedly innocent ignorance is not as plentiful as people like to imagine. Ignorance is more than just not knowing certain things. Ignoring is almost always a culpable and dangerous action – and the word is meaningless if the action of ignoring is not deliberate. Ignorance is consciously ignoring things we would rather not be bothered about – and being content *not* to find out, *not* to face facts, *not* to learn God's will, and *not* to follow certain right paths.

It should be obvious that admitting foolishness and ignorance is essential if we are to learn more and choose a better way.

Like a Beast
I was like a beast before You. (Psalm 73:22b)

This looks like a man kicking himself in unrelieved misery and self-pity. Asaph, however, is looking back and, as with his foolishness and ignorance, is reporting a sober observation he certainly did not discern at the time, but which, *ex post facto*, seems incontrovertible. He is saying: "In my stupidity and ignorance, I was no better than an animal." He is, however, no more saying he was an animal, than my mother – when she said to me, "You are stubborn as a mule." – was saying I really was a mule! Solomon points out that when people live only an "under the sun" life, they deny their humanity in the end, and behave as if they are no more than just another animal. "'Concerning the condition of the sons of men, God tests them, that they may see that they themselves are like animals.' For what happens to the sons of men also happens to animals; one thing befalls them: as one dies, so dies the other. Surely, they all have one breath; man has no advantage over animals, for all is vanity." (Eccl. 3:18-19). A modern evolutionist will say: "Yes, that's what humans are" – and plenty people live the life that Solomon is saying is actually a denial of the very purpose of the life God has given humankind.

Be sure of this: neither Solomon nor Asaph are saying we become "animals" when we sin. The point is that this is not what we really are, or what we will literally become. The key in v. 22b is in the expression "before You." It concerns what we are doing with our humanity *before* God. We are made in His image. Our purpose is, before Him, to bear His image in His Creation. We are accountable to Him, to walk in His way, to shine as lights in a dark place and to worship Him and glorify His Name. This is a high calling with profound purposes and glorious blessings in time and for eternity.

Remember the prodigal son. He wasted his inheritance in riotous living and ruined his life. When and how did he waken to reality? That was when he was dining in the pig's trough! He was, so to speak, no better than a pig, when he was meant to be his Father's son (Luke 15:11-32). Now, we are all God's offspring (Acts 17:28). But do we all live as such "before God"? Is this too hard? No, it is not. It is an essential pointer to godly honesty on the path to real life before the Lord. And it expresses loving aspiration for our souls as we "press toward the goal for the prize of the upward call of God in Christ Jesus." (Phil. 3:14).

Nevertheless

Nevertheless, I am continually with You;
You hold me by my right hand. (Psalm 73:23)

Matthew Henry calls this part of Psalm 73, "Samson's riddle again unriddled." You may remember from Judges 14:14 that the riddle was:

"Out of the eater came something to eat, and
out of the strong came something sweet." (Judges 14:14)

Samson had killed a lion and later had found honeycombs in its carcass. As applied to Asaph, it was to say that out of the "lion" of struggling with doubt and temptation, came "something sweet," namely the renewal of Asaph's wavering faith. From the sour taste of doubt came sweet fellowship with the Lord. O, to desire and experience such a happy outcome for ourselves, after dark trials and troubles!

In spite of provoking the Lord, the psalmist was not left indefinitely to his own devices. And the Lord never abandoned him, even when if He did allow him some time to dally with the rope that might have been enough to hang him, for all he knew. When he went into the Temple, to the worship of God, the Lord in His matchless grace showed him the desperate state of sinners, and their need of sacrifice for sin, if they were not to be justly plunged into a lost eternity (73:17-20). Asaph was compelled by God's grace to examine himself (v. 21); and he was convicted of his sin and transformed by the renewing of his mind (v. 22). The key word in our text, that encapsulates the essence of what the Lord did for him, is "nevertheless." It points to all the blessings of becoming and being a child of God (v. 23a).

"Nevertheless" is a marker of the real Christian, because it is this that makes, says Martyn Lloyd-Jones, "the whole difference between the Christian and the non-Christian."[19] It says "I was lost, 'nevertheless' I am now saved." Every real believer can and will say this. No non-believer can claim this – until and unless he is converted by and to Christ, and saved. Asaph – the sinning saint and back-sliding believer – is expressing the wonder of the forgiveness of sin and the restoration of reconciled communion with his Redeemer he once again enjoys. That glorious word – "nevertheless" – marks the difference saving grace makes in a sinner's life.

---

[19] M. Lloyd-Jones, *op. cit.*, 87.

It points to the real hope which is to be found exclusively in the Lord who saves and who does not abandon His people, no matter how low they may go.

Here is what this means, by way of application:

1. First of all, it is *all of God's grace*. Nobody is saved because he or she is either better, or a better prospect, than others. Asaph is kept by the power of God, not the superior character of Asaph. He was not saved in the first place by having more potential – than say, Jezebel, or by some innate religiosity, or a capacity to be good. Salvation – and persevering in the faith thereafter – is all of grace, undeserved and unearned.

2. Secondly, there is a God who is *faithful*. We are called to turn to Him, depend upon and conscientiously follow Him in the obedience of faith. But we are not turned to Him because of what we decide to do, as if we are independent and autonomous actors in the matter, or are merely acting in response to "ups and downs" or cyclical moods. No, all along, it is the Lord's "nevertheless" and "continually" that is the engine of our redemption, from regeneration to repentance and faith, to persevering faithfulness and running renewal, and finally to resurrection. All along our blessings are the fruit of His covenant faithfulness – whether we are awake or sleeping, when we are assailed by tests and trials, and even if we are caught up in the foolishness and ignorance of back-sliding. "Nevertheless" and "continually" call us to His promises and the response of godliness from us. He and remind us that, "He has not dealt with us according to our sins, nor punished us according to our iniquities." (Psalm 103:10), and that, "He who calls [us] is faithful, who also will do it." (1 The. 5:24). Our response, should be to act upon His enabling grace, for He promises us that: "If we confess our sins, He is faithful and just to forgive us our sins and to cleanse us from all unrighteousness." (1 John 1:9). Will we not then praise Him from the heart?: "If You, LORD, should mark iniquities, O Lord, who could stand?" (Psalm 130:3).

3. Thirdly, there is *a Savior* whose grace restrains and restores the troubled believer. Asaph testifies: "You hold me by my right hand." (v. 23b). Allow me a personal reference. The only memory I have of my Grandpa Keddie is of a walk he took me along the towpath of the

Union Canal in Edinburgh, Scotland, when I was about 5 years old. I wanted to be close to the water, to spot the Sticklebacks and Minnows. So Grandpa kindly held me by my right hand, in order to ensure I would not fall in. About twenty years later, by then a serious distance runner, I was on a training run on that same path, when I turned my ankle and fell badly – but to my right, away from the water. No Grandpa was there to hold my hand, but I was sure my Father in heaven was.

Will you look to the Lord to bear you up? Will you pray: "Uphold my steps in Your paths, that my footsteps may not slip" (Psalm 17:5)? Will you trust Him: "As for me, You uphold me in my integrity, and set me before Your face forever (Psalm 41:12)? Will you walk with Him: "My soul follows close behind You; Your right hand upholds me. (Psalm 63:8)? O, let us firmly hold right back to Christ with our right hand, and claim the promise He gives all who walk, or run (Heb. 12:1), or stumble in the Christian life: "Though he fall, he shall not utterly be cast down, for the Lord upholds him with His hand." (Psalm 37:24).

Chapter 6

Growth

You will guide me with Your counsel,
And afterward receive me to glory.
(Psalm 73:24)

"Momentum" is a popular word in everyday life. It began in 17th century physics, as descriptive of "force in motion. It is the product of the mass and velocity of a body. This has since been carried over to subjects such as politics, sport, business, warfare and even romance. If someone is succeeding – and seems to be "on the move" – we view this person as having "momentum," and we expect to see even more forward movement.

There can be something you might call "momentum" in the Christian life – and it concerns the experience of God's grace and spiritual growth in the discipleship of believers. The more we know of the nearness of God in the exercise of practical personal godliness - through union with Christ as our Savior and Lord, and the ministry of the Word, Sacraments and prayer – the more we discover a kind of spiritual momentum in our Christian lives.

You can see something of this in the flow of the text from verse 23 ("Nevertheless I am continually with You; You hold me by my right hand."); to verse 24: ("You will guide me with Your counsel, and afterward receive me to glory."). Here is a believer returning from backsliding, and growing in grace and the in knowledge of his Lord and Savior (2 Pet. 3:18). The Apostle John, speaking of the incarnate Christ, declares of believers that "of His fullness we have all received, and grace for grace." (John 1:16). This the logic of progressive sanctification – *grace upon grace* in the believer's new life in Jesus Christ. The engine of spiritual momentum is not sourced in our commitment, vision, or piety, but in the Gospel power of God to salvation in Christ (Rom. 1:16), applied in His work of grace in us by the indwelling Holy Spirit, whose "temple" each true believer is. There is an unmistakable momentum in the very nature of God's work of grace in human hearts. As Paul argues: "For if when we were enemies we were reconciled to God through the death of His Son, much more, having been reconciled, we shall be saved by His life." (Rom. 5:10); and "He who did not spare His own Son, but delivered Him up for us all, how shall He not with Him also freely give us all things?" (Rom. 8:32). With this in mind, we turn to Asaph's testimony in verse 24.

God Guides Us Now
You will guide me with Your counsel. (Psalm 73:24a)

On the dark night of May 20, 1962, a high school senior was going home on a bus winding through the hills of south-eastern Scotland. He was a bit sore from a five-a-side football (soccer) tournament that afternoon, but both exhilarated and pensive because in the evening Rally, under the preaching of Ecclesiastes 12:1*ff*, he had committed his way to Christ. At every bend of that twisting road, he could see the "cat's eyes" reflectors in the middle line, as they picked up the vehicle's headlights, and wondered where that line of lights might be leading him in his future life as a new Christian. He was just 17 and pondered what God would do with him. He also had not the first clue about that future.[20]

The psalmist wondered what his future held. We saw in his very experience of God's grace restoring him to faithfulness, that he was assured of the Lord's embracing him in revived fellowship. He is in renewed communion with the Lord and the Lord is holding him in refreshed union with Himself (v. 23). But what would that look like in the details? Tomorrow is always another day, and whatever we may have on our calendar, or propose to do with our time, the Lord's dispositions remain uncertain and inscrutable. But Asaph is immediately given a wonderful encouragement, to arm his soul with expectancy of good things for the future course of his life. There are four aspects to this promised blessing – which, please note, is extended to every believer without exception.

1. We *always* do not know the future. This first encouragement is one of the many "negatives" in the Bible that is actually a "positive." As Solomon says: Do not boast about tomorrow, for you do not know

---

[20] Over six decades later, he is writing these words.

what a day may bring forth." (Prov. 27:1). Hoping, planning and praying, in anticipation of what a day will bring forth, may often be followed by encouraging fulfilments, but hoping, planning and praying are not equivalent to knowing what will actually happen. A strong feeling that makes you sure you "know" is still a feeling and not a fact of divine revelation. If we knew the future, why would we hope, plan or pray? We cannot even predict what good and wise actions will have good and happy results. It was a good thing in itself that Joseph went to visit his brothers, but it got him slavery in Egypt and might have cost him his life. David visited his brothers, and it issued his unexpected killing of Goliath and the deliverance of Israel from Philistine bondage. The simple – and absolute – point is that life is uncertain at the best of times. Whatever we may *feel, suspect or think we know*, we actually do not know what a day may bring forth. It may seem paradoxical, but that is why hoping, planning and praying are what they are, and why they are important exercises of a living faith in the Lord who not only knows, but does all things well.

2. We are, however, *never* left by the Lord in the dark, so as to despond and despair without any relief. He will guide us with His counsel. In this we have precious and powerful *promise*s: "I will instruct you and teach you in the way you should go; I will guide you with My eye." (Psalm 32:8).

At first sight, this may seem a very curious characterization of either the source or content of "counsel." But we are certainly used to being guided by our own eyes, too often to our own detriment (*cf*, Psalm 36:1; 101:3; 119:37). And in our technological age, we routinely depend on that "eye in the sky," the satellite-fed GPS. God, however, has His eye upon us all the time, and for blessing: "Behold, the eye of the LORD is on those who fear Him, on those who hope in His mercy, to deliver their soul from death, and to keep them alive in famine." (Psalm 33:18-19).

Notice that this does not give us certain knowledge of the details and circumstances of His providence (nor does it, for example, encourage us to speculate about when Christ will come, or we will go!). It does encourage us to wait, praise, rejoice, trust, pray and hope in Him as our help, shield and deliverer: "Our soul waits for the LORD; He is our help and our shield. For our heart shall rejoice in Him, because we have trusted in His holy name. Let Your mercy, O LORD, be upon us, just as we hope in You." (Psalm 33:20-22). The Lord's eye is upon us and ahead of us, *seeing what we cannot see*, and decreeing what we can neither know nor guarantee. He is the bright eye in our sky – the seeing-eye God, who will see His beloved people through to the glory yet to be revealed.

We also have a *prayer*. Or we should say, we have the privilege of constant resort to the Lord in prayer that has the certainty of being heard. Why do we pray? Surely because we know God's promise and power – but also His purpose of love from all eternity. David, no stranger to feast and famine in his spiritual life, shows us how to pray: "Therefore, my spirit is overwhelmed within me; My heart within me is distressed. I remember the days of old; I meditate on all Your works; I muse on the work of Your hands. I spread out my hands to You; My soul *longs* for You like a thirsty land. Answer me speedily, O LORD; My spirit fails! Do not hide Your face from me, Lest I be like those who go down into the pit. Cause me to hear Your lovingkindness in the morning, For in You do I trust; Cause me to know the way in which I should walk, For I lift up my soul to You." (Psalm 143:4-8). The plea in Psalm 143 is from past mercies – and the Lord's known character and reputation – to future blessing. What He has done offers prospects of what He will yet do. Believing prayer is not a mere cry of pain, as if having been hit by a brick. It is an informed plea for help, succor and guidance from the One who is trusted as Savior and Lord.

We are, therefore, *persuaded* that He is faithful and able to keep His promises. Are we not his *believing* people? Asaph declares: "You will guide me with Your counsel." We have here what God will do and how He will do it.

1. "You will guide me…" is a confession of faith. Asaph believes God. If you don't believe Him, you can expect the heavens to be brass (Deut. 28:23), until you truly cry to Him in faith.
2. "…with Your counsel" is how the Lord guides the praying believer' This He does by His revealed truth - the word of the truth of the Bible (Psalm 119:105); and the ministry of "the Holy Spirit

speaking in the Scriptures."[21] The Spirit accompanies the Word with power and thereby leads us into all truth (John 16:13; *cf.* 14; 16, 25; 15:26).

Thomas Manton comments on Psalm 73:24: "We have it from God, and we have it from his word; for there is a guide and a rule. Man is so weak and so perverse that he needs both a guide and a rule. The guide is the Spirit of God, and the rule is the word of God: thou shalt guide me, but by thy counsel. By these two alone can we be led in the way to true happiness."[22]

God Will Bring Us Home
... and afterward receive me to glory. (Psalm 73:24b)

Glory is, as we have noted, the eternal destination of Heaven, into which God promises to receive His believing people. In every moment of human history, He is guiding His to their heavenly home – that "inheritance incorruptible and undefiled and that does not fade away, reserved in heaven for you, who are kept by the power of God through faith for salvation ready to be revealed in the last time." (1 Pet. 1:4). Salvation is first what we have been saved from – that is what came home to the psalmist after he went into the house of God – but salvation is also about what we are saved *to*. That is what is rejoicing the psalmist's soul. Why? Because this is where God's goodness is taking him, as He guides him with His counsel – and, we might add, helps him to negotiate the circumstances that had recently troubled him so grievously. Seeing what God is really doing for him – from Day One – transforms his view of the fallen world and his own life and destiny.

Listen, believer! Even being thankful to the Lord for these mercies does not rise to the full measure of God's grace in our salvation. Glorifying God is the ultimate expression of the soul that is saved! Matthew Henry has a beautiful comment on v. 24b: "If we make God's glory *in us* the end we aim at, he will make our glory *with him* the end we shall be forever happy in."[23] It is of course a wonderful thing to know Christ Jesus as your Savior. And it is marvelously encouraging to see His works of grace in hearts and lives

---

[21] Westminster Confession of Faith, I.x.
[22] Thomas Manton, *Complete Works*, Vol. VI: 230.
[23] M. Henry, *op. cit.*, Vol. III: 515.

in the course of our lives, and have such reasons to give thanks to Him. How much more will we glory in the Lord in prospect of soon being with Him in Glory? O, think often of Heaven. We are not long here. And strive earnestly for Heaven, and you will be all the more blessed on Earth. Look at what He has done and is doing for those He is saving to Himself:

1. *God's love is "an everlasting love" – from eternity to eternity.* He tells us: "Yes, I have loved you with an everlasting love; Therefore with lovingkindness I have drawn you." (Jer. 31:3). His love is not merely longer and larger in scope than the on-off and stop-start devotion we children of Adam are oft-times pleased to call love. God did not wake up one morning and decide to love people and send His Son to save them. "Everlasting" did not start some day after Adam and Eve fell. It never started and it never will end. We who are time-bound, think of eternity-past and eternity-future, but in the mind of the infinite-eternal God, it is all one. Furthermore, God does not decide to love and save certain folk because He is suddenly moved one day as He sees they are going through a bad time. No, God loves particularly from the beginning – and there is no "variation or shadow of turning" with Him (Jas. 1:17). God's Word explains with crystal clarity: "Blessed be the God and Father of our Lord Jesus Christ, who has blessed us with every spiritual blessing in the heavenly places in Christ, just as He chose us in Him before the foundation of the world, that we should be holy and without blame before Him in love, having predestined us to adoption as sons by Jesus Christ to Himself, according to the good pleasure of His will, to the praise of the glory of His grace, by which He has made us accepted in the Beloved." (Eph. 1:3-6).

2. *God has a purpose of grace in His love.* If the psalmist had not realized before his doubt and declension that God's love and grace were entirely of His initiation and implementation – and wholly undeserved and unearned by the sinner – he surely understood after his restoration that he was saved by God's free grace and not by any righteous of his own. Far less did he imagine that any of his sufferings could ever atone for a scintilla of his sin. The New Testament reveals the glory and fulness of Christ as the Messiah foretold and prefigured in the Old. God "so loved the world that He gave His only begotten Son, that whoever believes in Him should not perish but have everlasting life. For God did not send

His Son into the world to condemn the world, but that the world through Him might be saved." (John 3:16-17). This presupposes that "a man is not justified by the works of the law but by faith in Jesus Christ, even we have believed in Christ Jesus, that we might be justified by faith in Christ and not by the works of the law; for by the works of the law no flesh shall be justified." (Gal. 2:16).

God "demonstrates His own love toward us, in that while we were still sinners, Christ died for us." (Rom. 5:8). Christ Jesus is the One "who was delivered up because of our offenses, and was raised because of our justification." (Rom. 4:25), and it is alone "by grace you have been saved through faith, and that not of yourselves; it is the gift of God, not of works, lest anyone should boast. For we are His workmanship, created in Christ Jesus for good works, which God prepared beforehand that we should walk in them." (Eph. 2:8-10).

God also gives us a glorious glimpse of His eternal purpose to save lost sinners: "For whom He foreknew, He also predestined to be conformed to the image of His Son, that He might be the firstborn among many brethren." (Rom. 8:29).

3. *God secures the salvation of His people* (Matt. 1:21). He guarantees His saving work in all that He saves. Too many Christians think that "getting saved" is a one-off act of conversion engineered by the Lord and agreed to by us, from which we go on to the Christian life in which if we do things right, the Lord will bless us. Scripture views God's gracious work of salvation as life-long and enquiring the supernatural work of the indwelling Holy Spirit constantly leading us into all truth. Sanctification is not a one-off either, but is, as the Westminster *Shorter Catechism* 35 so beautifully describes it: "the work of God's free grace, whereby we are renewed in the whole man after the image of God, and are enabled more and more to die unto sin, and live unto righteousness." The renewing is a "more and more" enabling; a lifetime of spiritual growth and persevering in the faith until we come to the completion of our salvation, in Glory.

We are not our own at any point in this "work of God's free grace." It is true that we are to "work out [our] own salvation with fear and trembling," but that cannot happen apart from God working in us "both to will and to do for His good pleasure." (Phil. 2:12-13). Our doubts and declension ought to teach us we cannot go it alone, even for a day. The watchword for fighting "the good fight of faith" (1 Tim. 6:12) is not "self-reliance" but being "continually" with the Lord, your right hand held by Him as He guides you with His counsel every day in life. The Apostle Peter pronounces the blessing upon walking with the Lord: "Grace and peace be multiplied to you in the knowledge of God and of Jesus our Lord, as His divine power has given to us all things that pertain to life and godliness, through the knowledge of Him who called us by glory and virtue, by which have been given to us exceedingly great and precious promises, that through these you may be partakers of the divine nature, having escaped the corruption that is in the world through lust." (2 Pet. 1:2-4).

We are not only not alone, but are united to Christ. The Apostle Paul points out that, "just as Christ was raised from the dead by the glory of the Father, even so we also should walk in newness of life." He drives this home: "For if we have been united together in the likeness of His death, certainly we also shall be in the likeness of His resurrection, knowing this, that our old man was crucified with Him, that the body of sin might be done away with, that we should no longer be slaves of sin." (Rom. 6:4-6).

We can have assurance of persevering in Christ, by His grace, "being confident of this very thing, that He who has begun a good work in [us] will complete it until the day of Jesus Christ." (Phil. 1:6; *cf.* Rom. 8:33-39). The Apostle Paul assures the faithful believers: "we have peace with God through our Lord Jesus Christ, through whom also we have access by faith into this grace in which we stand, and rejoice in hope of the glory of God. And not only that, but we also glory in tribulations, knowing that tribulation produces perseverance; and perseverance, character; and character, hope. Now hope does not disappoint, because the love of God has been poured out in our hearts by the Holy Spirit who was given to us." (Rom. 5:1-5).

Expect Blessing

We are encouraged by God to *expect blessing.* There is an inseparable connection between heeding His counsel *now* and being received into the "glory" which is heaven, *"afterward."* Christ truly in us is the hope of glory (Col. 1:27; Rom. 5:2). Faith in Christ is not a substitute for obedience to His will. Faith is the engine of obedience and obedience is the evidence of faith. Yet we all know very well that the expectation of entering heaven when we die far outstrips credible evidence of living faith in the Lord Jesus Christ and a discernable concomitant enthusiasm for God's Word in many who say they are Christians. Ignoring God's counsel, and imagining you are saved and will go to heaven, is just that – imagining. "Faith without works is dead." (Jas. 2:20). No faith at all is unvarnished enmity with God (Heb. 11:6; Rom. 8:7).

The promise of God always – and obviously – implies the anticipation of blessing from Him. As He guides us, and we follow Him heart and hands, we can expect to arrive at His destination for us. And along that way, the practice of godliness carries with it the growing experience of a deepening communion with the Lord. This all points us to our personal walk with the Lord. John says, "Every man who has this hope in him purifies himself." (1 John 3:3). What hope? Hope in Christ and, in Him, the hope of the glory of an eternal inheritance with Him. This is progressive sanctification in exercise, in which we will take hold of the Lord's encouragements. And "lay aside every weight, and the sin which so easily ensnares us, and ... run with endurance the race that is set before us, looking unto Jesus, the author and finisher of our faith, who for the joy that was set before Him endured the cross, despising the shame, and has sat down at the right hand of the throne of God." (Heb. 12:1).

"And the Lord will deliver me from every evil work and preserve me for His heavenly kingdom. To Him be glory forever and ever. Amen!" (2 Tim. 4:18).

Chapter 7

The Desire of Your Heart

"Whom have I in heaven but You?"
(Psalm 73:25)

We make choices in life every waking hour. In matters great and small, we choose what is most important at least in our own estimation. We can be right; we can be wrong; and the consequences, in both cases, can be anything from wonderful to woeful. It isn't simply about "bad" people making bad choices and "good" people making good choices, but about people (sinners saved and unsaved) making decisions that are sometimes bad, sometimes good and sometimes both in quick succession. We can go back and forth in our choices. John Erskine (1675-1732), was the Earl of Mar and some-time Secretary of State for Scotland. His nickname was "Bobbing John," because he "bobbed" from Whig to Tory, and Jacobite to Hanoverian. His priority was being on the winning side. Priorities determine choices. They reveal the deeper desires of the heart.

Everybody has heart-desires and priorities of some kind. There are athletes who live for sport; movie stars who aim for fame; people obsessed with hobbies; and workaholics who neglect their families. There are vivid examples in the Bible: Jonadab loved getting people into trouble (2 Sam. 13); The rich young man loved his wealth (Luke 18:18-24); the prodigal son lived for fun and frolic (Luke 15:11-21); Jezebel was devoted to false gods and murdering people (1 Ki. 16:31; 18:4); Noah was a preacher of righteousness (2 Pet. 2:5); Jesus was always about His Father's business (Luke 2:49). "In religion," wrote Thomas Watson, "the heart is all. If the heart be not turned from sin, it is no better than a lie."[24] The psalmist would

---

[24] T. Watson, *The Doctrine of Repentance* (Edinburgh: Banner of Truth, 1999 [1668]), 53. Thomas Watson (1620-86) was an English "Puritan" preacher and one of most luminous Christian writers of his time. Many of his books have been in print to this day.

certainly have agreed, for he had just wrestled with his own heart and his personal relationship to the Living God. Asaph is, of course, a case in point. He is a believer, yet he toyed with unbelief. He swithered over changing the whole direction in his thinking and living, and hovered on the brink of apostasy from his Lord. His choices reflect his wavering priorities and allegiances. We have seen, in 73:18-24, how he came to understand the real issue and what was at stake. He admitted his foolishness and ignorance, and re-affirmed his faith. Charles Simeon notes that in "his more deliberate judgment, he determines to take God as his only portion."[25] Now in 73:25 we have a remarkable testimony from the psalmist, in which God is calling us to examine our hearts as to what desires and priorities define our personal relationship to Him and drive our decision-making in daily life. Asaph highlights two basic aspects about his heart's desire, which also apply you and to me.

Whom Have You in Heaven?
Whom have I in heaven but You… (Psalm 73:25a)

This may remind you of Peter's words in John 6:68. A number of Jesus's followers had abandoned Him because of His teaching on the "bread from heaven." (v. 58). Jesus asks the Twelve if they also will leave Him. Peter replies vigorously: "Lord, to whom shall we go?", giving as his reason: "You have the words of eternal life." (v. 68).

Martyn Lloyd-Jones thinks that Asaph's, "whom have I in heaven but you…," is by way of contrast a bit negative in the language used, since he says nothing explicitly positive about God. Lloyd-Jones takes this to indicate some hesitancy in his commitment.[26] But surely it is the language of surrender? How could it be more positive, coming from someone who has just confessed he came close to leaving God altogether? Neither Asaph nor Peter has a grudging tone, as if to say – glumly – "What alternative do I have?" No! This is a humble but exultant confiding in the Lord.

---

[25] C. Simeon, *Expository Outlines on the Whole Bible* (Grand Rapids, MI: Baker, 1988 [1847]), Vol. 6:15. Charles Simeon (1759-1836) was, for over half a century, the renowned Anglican evangelical pastor of Holy Trinity Church, Cambridge. He is regarded as one of the greatest expositors of Scripture in the English-speaking world and his 21 volume *Expository Outlines* is still available, giving eloquent testimony to his gifts as a preacher.

[26] M. Lloyd-Jones, *op. cit.*, 107-108.

Why the focus on heaven?

Surely it is to move us to ask ourselves where we think salvation actually comes from: "To whom must I go, can I go to find a Savior – even in heaven? Not to angels, or to the already saved saints of the Lord! I can go only to the One who has the words of eternal life! But why "in heaven"? There are a couple of important considerations here:

1. The Savior of sinners is divine: the God who is "in Christ reconciling the world to Himself" (2 Cor. 5:19). This is what unfolds in both Testaments of Scripture, the shadows of the Old and the substance of the New. "For there is one God, and one mediator between God and men, the man Christ Jesus." (1 Tim. 2:5). Preachers and Popes save no one. Pilgrimages to so-called "holy places" save no one. Phenomenal religious ritual saves no one. Pious thoughts save no one. Your best works cannot save you. "God alone" can "forgive sins" (Luke 5:21).

2. If we are to be *spiritually healed*, there is no one on earth who is able to effect it. When you need physical healing, you go to a doctor's office, or a hospital, for the necessary treatment. But there is no religious functionary, even if he is the most godly and gifted minister of God, who can actually do the healing in this world. The church, if it has a sound ministry, can, must and will point you to the Lord who saves in the regular "means of grace," but the actual healing comes from heaven and is ministered by the Holy Spirit in your heart, as He accompanies the Word which has been ministered to your heart, mind, and soul (Matt. 22:37).

3. The salvation of a soul is a *supernatural work* of the One we have in heaven, and you will only get it from heaven, for that is where the Savior is, and is the place from which His salvation is administered to us in this world. Another psalmist records: "He sent from above, He took me; He drew me out of many waters. He delivered me …" (Psalm 18:16-17). Conversion to Christ, victory over sin and trials, and spiritual growth are not merely internal actions we perform within ourselves. They are not just intellectual transactions, and certainly are not accomplished by emotional catharses. It requires distinct works of the Holy Spirit to regenerate a stony heart (Eze. 11:19). It takes a day of God's power to make someone willing to repent, believe in, and

follow Jesus (Psalm 110:3). It takes looking away from ourselves, and whatever resources we may think we have, and reaching, as it were, all the way to heaven, to God, Father, Son and Holy Spirit, for the application of all the resources of Gospel grace – the power of God to salvation for all who will believe (Rom. 1:16). We are never left to ourselves. The Lord *is* doing in us and for us more than we can ask and think – or even are aware of (Eph. 3:20).

Confessing faith and heaven

Confessing faith is, in Matthew Henry's lively words, "the workings and breathings of a soul toward God."[27] Where are these "workings and breathings" going? They go to heaven! Actually, we may say they also *begin* in heaven with the Lord. And this says something about all our choices and heart's-desires – including what we believe and what we do. These *need* to be sourced out of Glory, from the Lord. "For who in the heavens can be compared to the LORD? Who among the sons of the mighty can be likened to the LORD?" (Psalm 89:6). "If then you were raised with Christ, seek those things which are above, where Christ is, sitting at the right hand of God. Set your mind on things above, not on things on the earth. (Col. 3:1-2).

The second clause of 73:25 shows us how Asaph's heavenward focus impacted his perspective on planet earth.

Nothing Upon Earth?

And there is nothing upon earth that I desire besides you." (Psalm 73:25b ESV)

God and heaven put this world in proper perspective. Asaph realized, in Lloyd-Jones's words, that "when he was wrong with God, he was wrong everywhere."[28] The psalmist was tempted by "the prosperity of the wicked" because he stopped delighting in God and desiring His guidance in his life, and was drawn to worldly success and material comforts. If you live in the conviction of an "under the sun" world-view, you will choose this world every time. That is what worldliness is: this world as a closed system, with no God, no heaven – and you hope – no hell. After his exposure to the

---

[27] M. Henry, *op. cit.*, Vol. III: 516.
[28] M. Lloyd-Jones, *op. cit.*, 108.

meaning of the sacrifices of the Temple, and no doubt the influence of the types and shadows of the Redeemer in the Feasts, the Ordinances and even the Furniture prescribed in God's Law,[29] Asaph saw the folly of his attraction to the "broken cisterns" of worldly standards of prosperity and the good life (Jer. 3:20).

Desire for the Lord

The point is that Asaph's desire is for the Lord Himself. His love for the Lord is not what used to be called "cupboard love" – what you can get out of it. He does not desire God even for what God can do for him – providing forgiveness, prosperity, health, self-esteem, personal satisfaction, &etc. His problem before was to complain about what God was *not* doing for him *versus* what He seemed to be doing for total unbelievers! Now, he desires fellowship with God Himself – a personal walk and intimate communion with the personal Redeemer-God. This is the desire that worships the Lord in spirit and in truth (John 4:24). This is the desire that denies all idols of the heart and mind that tempt us to a false worship.

The Bible is so clear on this aspiration of those who are truly committed to the Lord:

1. "As the deer pants for the water brooks, so pants my soul for You, O God. My soul thirsts for God, for the living God. When shall I come and appear before God?" (Psalm 42:1-2).
2. "…that I may know Him and the power of His resurrection, and the fellowship of His sufferings, being conformed to His death" (Phil. 3:10).
3. "And this is eternal life, that they may know You, the only true God, and Jesus Christ whom You have sent." (John 17:3).
4. "'You shall love the LORD your God with all your heart, with all your soul, and with all your mind.' This is the first and great commandment. And the second is like it: 'You shall love your neighbor as yourself.'" (Matt. 22:37-39).

---

[29] For a wonderful and accessible exposition of these "types and shadows," all later fulfilled in Christ and the Gospel, see the modern edition of the classic work by William McEwen, *The Glory and Fulness of Jesus Christ* (Grand Rapids: Reformation Heritage Books, 2022 [1763]).

Does God Really Care About Me?

Is this the desire of your heart?

Plenty people talk about "believing in God" – and even "accepting" Jesus – but it seems to make little impact on their lives. Sure, there is someone "out there" or "up there," and they agree with by impenetrably vague generalities. But is that anything more credible than the "faith" James challenges when he says to some who think they are Christians: "You believe that there is one God. You do well. Even the demons believe – and tremble!" (Jas. 2:19). Asaph, however, believes with a deep personal interest in his Lord. He loves Him from the heart, and that moves his decisions, his aspirations, his hopes, his expectations – his whole life! How do we *know* God? The full answer is: in Jesus Christ. "He has made known the Father" (John 10:38). We see God (the Father) "in the face of Jesus Christ" (2 Cor. 4:6). And Jesus tells us, "He who has seen Me, has seen the Father" (John 14:7). We come to the Father through Jesus the Son. And so, when we believe upon Christ as our Savior and are received and accepted by Him, we too may say, "Whom have I in heaven but You?" Then we will know in our hearts that there is nothing upon earth that we desire besides Him, and that we are for sure in His hands.

———————

Chapter 8

The Strength of Your Heart

My flesh and my heart fail;
But God is the strength of my heart
and my portion forever.
(Psalm 73:26)

Does it seem incongruous that just after the psalmist affirms his revitalized faith in God in the glorious words, "There is nothing on earth that I desire besides You…" (v. 25b), he immediately goes on to say: "My flesh and my heart fail." (v. 26a)? It seems a strange moment at which – in the words of the song of ante-bellum slaves – "Sometimes I'm up" should meet "Sometimes I'm down." Could Asaph not have gone straight to the marvelous pæan that follows: "… God is the strength of my heart and my portion forever." (v. 26b)? Why even mention his spiritual heart failure at all? Is it not enough for him for him to express his gratitude and encouragement in the Lord's restoring his soul (Psalm 23:3)?

The most obvious answer, surely, is that he needs to confess that before the Lord brought him to desire nothing on earth above Him, he had a deep problem of desiring a lot of things on earth quite a bit more than he desired God! All his envy of the "prosperity of the wicked" emanated from this root. We need not labor the point, but we do need to understand that the psalmist, under the inspiration of the Holy Spirit, mentions the failure of flesh and heart, first, to make clear both his sin and God's victory in him, and, second, to direct us to face this issue in our own lives. We too can go off course into spiritual backslidings. We too can drift away from the Lord, from the word of truth, from the obedience of faith, from personal and practical fellowship with Him, and so become cold in our love for Him and for His way. Jesus says of these last days: "And because lawlessness will abound, the love of many will grow cold." (Matt. 24:12). Asaph's words are God's words for embattled and failing hearts. He offers us four ways in which God supplies His solutions to the problem. He is the provider, the perfector, the preserver, and the portion forever of the believer's life.

Provider

The need is, of course, in the psalmist's evaluation of himself: "my flesh and my heart fail." Are we not all persuaded by our own experience that this is not infrequently true to life?

The "flesh" is always failing. Every little pain proves that. Sickness, aging and death all point to this reality. "Flesh," meaning the body, succumbs eventually. That word "flesh" also refers in Scripture to our corruptible nature, as, for example, in Galatians 5:13: "do not use liberty as an opportunity for the flesh," and 1 John 2:16: "the lust of the flesh." There is an endemic weakness in us all – and with it comes the ongoing assumption of the need of saving strength and upholding grace.

The "heart" intensifies both the need and the solution. The "heart" represents the center of our being – that "inner man" of Ephesians 3:16, that is "deceitful above all things, and desperately sick, who can understand it."

What then is our Lord's provision for this endemic threat? It is strength that we cannot come up with from our own resources. Many Christians, alas, react to their patent weaknesses with little more than a shrug of resignation - it's the way I am, and I can't change it. They will then apologetically invoke a postdated forgiveness from a generous God, as if it excuses present and future sin they expect to go on committing, and otherwise do nothing to rectify. Every pastor has seen this in his ministry, and perhaps every Christian has practiced this defeatism at some time in his life. Over against that, we have numerous encouragements to fight the good fight in dependence upon the Lord's enabling grace:

1. Psalm 18:32 – "It is God who arms me with strength, and makes my way perfect."
2. Psalm 29:11 – "The LORD will give strength to His people; The LORD will bless His people with peace."
3. Psalm 138:3 – "In the day when I cried out, You answered me, and made me bold with strength in my soul."

All and every sense of weakness should send us crying confidently to our Savior, who provides powerfully for His people from His bountiful grace: "But those who wait on the LORD Shall renew *their* strength; They shall mount up with wings like eagles. They shall run and not be weary. They shall walk and not faint." (Isa. 40:31). Here is the issue, from Asaph to every one of us. Are you calling upon the Lord?

Perfector

Growth in grace is growth in strength. This is true, notwithstanding our feeling that weakness seems to cling to us and never go away. Asaph knew he had failed badly at least once, and understood that he would need all the help he could get to strive against whatever future temptations might touch him. It is not for nothing that we are called in the New Testament to, "Put on the whole armor of God, that you may be able to stand against the wiles of the devil." (Eph. 6:11). The Apostle Peter prays: "… may the God of all grace, who called us to His eternal glory by Christ Jesus, after you have suffered a while, perfect, establish, strengthen, and settle you." (1 Pet. 5:10). This is an instance of the overcoming, prevailing faith recorded throughout Hebrews 11. We do have the promise: "Resist the devil and he will flee from you." (Jas. 4:7). Resistance can be desperately exacting and it would be a great mistake to think we can shoo him away in our own strength.

The Apostle Paul was assailed by personal affliction that made him feel weak – the mysterious "thorn in the flesh." This appears to have been a physical weakness, not a spiritual failure. But the latter is often triggered by the former and it is not unlikely that Paul was deeply discouraged by that "thorn." He asked the Lord, (only) three times, that He remove it. Paul records the Lord's reply and his own response: "And He said to me, 'My grace is sufficient for you, for My strength is made perfect in weakness.' Therefore most gladly I will rather boast in my infirmities, that the power of Christ may rest upon me." (2 Cor. 12:9). Paul's application is along three lines:

1. He is content to "boast" in his weakness – but does not complain about it.
2. He is glad for his weakness – but refuses to be depressed or resentful about it.

3. He sees his weakness as an amazing occasion of Christ's power resting on him.

Paul sums up the experiential fruit that this is bearing in his soul: "Therefore I take pleasure in infirmities, in reproaches, in necessities, in persecutions, in distresses for Christ's sake: for when I am weak, then am I strong." (2 Cor. 12:10). It is not that he *wants* to be weak, or *chooses* to be weak – it is that in bringing his weakness before the Lord in faith, he experiences Christ's power to keep him and grow him. There is a universal application to us all in our awareness of weakness, physical and spiritual: in the face of our weaknesses are we laying down, or looking up? Are you striving in the Lord?

Preserver

But we are changeable. Personal victory seems too often to be dogged by personal defeat. When Asaph ponders spiritual heart failure, this is not to be dismissed as some "fear of failure" he needs to "snap out of." Neither is it to be regarded as a comment on his past failure, as if he will never face such a temptation or trial again. He is clearly declaring the ground for the necessity of God continuing to strengthen him along life's way.

Paul's experience in Romans 7:13-25 is relevant here. He is a mature believer, growing in grace. But with that, he is also all the more sensitive to sin as it is indwelling him. Until we are made perfect in holiness – in heaven – we will always live in the Romans 7-8 experience – in spiritual warfare, but with growing victory.

"For I delight in the law of God according to the inward man. [23] But I see another law in my members, warring against the law of my mind, and bringing me into captivity to the law of sin which is in my members. [24] O wretched man that I am! Who will deliver me from this body of death? [25] I thank God – through Jesus Christ our Lord! So then, with the mind I myself serve the law of God, but with the flesh the law of sin. [8:1] *There is* therefore now no condemnation to those who are in Christ Jesus, who do not walk according to the flesh, but according to the Spirit. [2] For the law of the Spirit of life in Christ Jesus has made me free from the law of sin and death. [3] For what the law could not do in that it was weak through the flesh, God *did* by sending His own Son in the likeness of sinful flesh, on account of sin: He condemned sin in the flesh, [4] that the righteous requirement of the law might be fulfilled in us who do not walk according to the flesh but according to the Spirit." (Rom. 7:20 – 8:4). *Our perseverance is guaranteed by Christ our Preserver:*

1. Psalm 63:7 – "Because You have been my help, therefore in the shadow of Your wings I will rejoice." That is, the God who perfects us, also empowers us to persevere. He preserves His gains in our Christian lives.
2. Psalm 91:1 – "He who dwells in the secret place of the Most High Shall abide under the shadow of the Almighty." Our active union and communion with the Lord will be our preservation by His grace in deepening fellowship with Him.
3. Colossians 3:3 – "For you died, and your life is hidden with Christ in God." As the Lord preserves us – provides, perfects and preserves the "strength of my heart," we experience that surrounding grace and enabling support in a sense of His nearness, His love for us, and His unfolding purpose of bringing us to Glory.

The practical issue of all of this is the fulfilment in our souls of that wonderful promise of the Lord: "You will keep him in perfect peace, whose mind is stayed on You, because he trusts in You." (Isa. 26:3). Will you intentionally, "Rest in the LORD, and wait patiently for Him" and "… not fret because of him who prospers in his way, because of the man who brings wicked schemes to pass."? (Psalm 37:7). O, embrace the Lord as the strength of your heart!

Portion Forever

The force of all of God's strengthening of our heart (providing, perfecting and preserving strength), is to deepen our awareness that we belong to the Lord – and that He belongs to us. Asaph exults: 'God is … my portion forever."

"My portion" takes the language of *inheritance* and applies it to our present relationship with the Lord, and our future destiny in eternity. He is our inheritance. Unlike earthly inheritances from our previous generations, He is the gift that gives now and without end, calling us "to an inheritance incorruptible and undefiled and that does not fade away, reserved in heaven for you, who are kept by the power of God through faith for salvation ready to be revealed in the last time." (1 Pet. 1:4).

The Lord is also "forever" our portion. Even now, this is a living and eternal consciousness of God's love, which can only rejoice our heart and empower our faithfulness to our glorious Savior: "You will show me the path of life; In Your presence *is* fullness of joy; At Your right hand *are* pleasures forevermore." (Psalm 16:11).

Here is the answer to declining strength and failing hearts. Not a longer, healthier, less troubled life here on this Earth, but a deepening walk with God that discovers love, grace and power in Christ as our hope of Heaven (Col. 1:5, 27). The issue concerns knowing the Lord in "the power of His resurrection, and the fellowship of His sufferings, being conformed to His death, if, by any means, I may attain to the resurrection from the dead." (Phil. 3:10-11) – and so, growing us all the way to Glory!

> *"My flesh and my heart fail;*
> *But God is the strength of my heart*
> *and my portion forever."*

Chapter 9

Draw Near to God

For indeed, those who are far from You shall perish; You have destroyed all those who desert You for harlotry. ^{28} *But it is good for me to draw near to God; I have put my trust in the Lord GOD, That I may declare all Your works.* (Psalm 73:27-28)

    A faith tried and found wanting doesn't seem worth the bother. That was the basic issue for Asaph underlying his doubting God's goodness. His faith was tested because he looked at the world and saw unbelieving people living rich and dying easy, while he was a believer and yet all he saw in his life was trouble (73:3-14). If God was blessing him, he had a hard time seeing it. So, he was edging towards giving up on God. It is always a temptation when someone seems to be letting you down.

    God, however, does not let him go. When Asaph went to the house of God, he evidently led Asaph to rethink. The result was that he was convicted of his foolishness, repented of his backsliding, and reaffirmed his faith in his Redeemer-God. He acknowledges his weakness (vv. 21-22), confesses God's kindness in sticking with him when he was tempted (v. 23), and commits afresh to the Lord for the future (vv. 24-26). What remains is the question: How he will actually behave in his refreshed faith in the Living God? What course will he bind himself to follow, in practice?

    God is giving the psalmist a fresh start, as indeed life must and always will have after spiritual renewal and forgiveness of sin. Verses 27-28 summarize his story and its practical implications, and set forth what the Lord calls all of us to do with our lives: "For indeed, those who are far from You shall perish; You have destroyed all those who desert You for harlotry. But it is good for me to draw near to God; I have put my trust in the Lord GOD, That I may declare all Your works." (Psalm 73:27). In New Testament fulness, this is the Gospel call to believe upon the Lord Jesus Christ and be saved (Acts 16:31; Rom. 10:9). And this is not the nod-and-a-wink nominalism of those who think themselves somehow right with God, but, as He says, only "draw near with their mouths and honor Me with their lips, but have removed their hearts far from Me, and their fear toward Me is taught by the commandment of men" (Isa. 29:13).

The Issue is Your Distance from God

Nothing had changed in the psalmist's external circumstances. He was still poor and the wicked were still prosperous. He had not come into money. God had not miraculously lifted his hardships in life. So, what *had* changed? What made the difference? Simply this: Asaph had come to see what was really important in his life, and it had to do with the nearness of God – God's acceptance of him – and his personal experience of nearness to God. The point is, as Martyn Lloyd-Jones puts it, "We are all either far from God or near to Him."[30] What dawned on Asaph was that *this* is the most important question in life. If you are *far* from God, you are in the deepest trouble in the universe! Being near to God – in faith and obedience – had for a time struck Asaph as not worth the bother. That was because prosperity, well-being and the comforts of life loomed large in his mind and assumed a (false) importance in his thinking. For a season he couldn't see past envying the wicked, and he drifted away from the God in whom he truly believed. Then he came to realize that being far from God is decidedly dangerous and potentially eternally lethal.

Here is the issue for believers and unbelievers alike – what is your distance from the Lord? You will hopefully have had cause to remember that, when you were little, you had parents and others who cared for you, kept an eye on you, and wanted you to keep close to them, especially in a crowd. It was to prevent you from losing your way and being exposed to all sorts of dangers. Asaph blesses God who holds his right hand. David praises God for taking his people under His wings: "How precious is Your lovingkindness, O God! Therefore the children of men put their trust under the shadow of Your wings." (Psalm 36:7). Jesus employs the same figure of speech as He laments over apostate Jerusalem: "O Jerusalem, Jerusalem, the one who kills the prophets and stones those who are sent to her! How often I wanted to gather your children together, as a hen gathers her chicks under her wings, but you were not willing!" (Matt. 23:37).

---

[30] M. Lloyd-Jones, *op. cit.*, 117.

As you read this, how close to the Lord are you in your heart, and in your daily walk with Him? Do you even feel the need to be close to God? Millions don't. "There is no fear of God before their eyes." (Rom. 3:18). "But," warns Solomon, "it will not be well with the wicked; nor will he prolong his days, which are as a shadow, because he does not fear before God. (Eccl. 8:13). Asaph knows his answer.

The Result of Being Far from God
For indeed, those who are far from You shall perish;
You have destroyed all those who desert You for harlotry. (Psalm 73:27)

It is obvious that if God is not in your life, there will sooner or later be definite consequences. Your life will prove that fact in all sorts of ways in God's timing, and with varying results in this life, but with only one of two in the end, when, as Daniel so solemnly reminds us, "… those who sleep in the dust of the earth shall awake, Some to everlasting life, Some to shame and everlasting contempt." (Dan. 12:2). The psalmist cuts to the chase…

Unbelief

Unbelief means you have stiff-armed the Lord, so that He is where you want Him to be – far from *you*. Short of a complete turn-about, the result will be cataclysmic and final: "For indeed, those who are far from [the Lord] shall perish." (v. 27a).

This perishing is the *natural* result of keeping God out of your life; that is, being without a saving knowledge of God in and through His Son, Jesus Christ. If you "put up the shutters" to Christ and the Gospel, you will ruin yourself in the end and forever (cf. John 3:18). Asaph is saying he will never be taken in again by the prosperity of the godless, for that is temporary and illusory. The Lord who saves is the One that we need (1 Tim. 2:5).

Apostasy

Apostasy refers to those who once professed to follow the Lord, but have chosen to "desert [God] for harlotry." Here, Asaph looks to history: "You *have* destroyed all those." (v. 27b) – those, that is, who fell away and never came back. They may have looked like saints – and convinced us all and themselves that they were right with God – but they did not persevere, and proved in reality to have been unconverted all along. The psalmist is saying that what has happened in the past, will happen in the future:

specifically, that there will be "covenant people" who fall away and of whom it may be said: "They went out from us, but they were not of us; for if they had been of us, they would have continued with us; but they went out that they might be made manifest, that none of them were of us." (1 John 2:19). Look at the history of Old Testament Israel and the New Testament Church – and the rolls of the membership and the covenant children of your local church! You know that the psalmist is thinking of himself here and what might have happened to him, without God's saving grace. His feet almost slipped. He envied the boastful. But by God's grace, he was enabled to hold God's hand and drew near to Him.

The Rewards of Drawing Near to God

But it is good for me to draw near to God;
I have put my trust in the Lord GOD,
That I may declare all Your works. (Psalm 73:28)

Drawing near to the Lord will transform your life. There are four principal components of this in the record of Asaph's testimony:

1. The blessing of the God of all grace: "But it is good for me to draw near to God." This is, of course, the reversal of what happens when you keep God out of your life and so deliberately draw away from Him. David declares: "Blessed is the man You choose, and cause to approach You, that he may dwell in Your courts. We shall be satisfied with the goodness of Your house, of Your holy temple." (Psalm 65:4). From the new convert to the aged saint, and with the returning back-slider, there is grace abounding to the chief of sinners in every heart that draws near to the Lord.

2. The affirmation of saving faith: "I have put my trust in the Lord God." This, too, represents a reversal of Asaph's questioning of his earlier faith and trust in the Lord. His renewed trust also rings with the sweet tones of true assurance of faith, echoing the previous verse: "God is the strength of my heart and my portion forever." (v. 26).

3. The joy of personal testimony: "That I may declare…" is also a reversal of his sinful unhappiness with God, and follows up his repentant reaffirmation of God as his Redeemer: "Whom have I in heaven but You? And there is none upon earth that I desire besides You." (v. 25).

He is restored to the joy of his salvation, and could sing with David: "I will sing of the mercies of the LORD forever; With my mouth will I make known Your faithfulness to all generations." (Psalm 89:1).

4. The glory of God in His works: "… all Your works" reverses complaints that God had not done all things well. Now, Asaph understands the perfection of God's sovereignty over all circumstances, even when some are hard providences. There is content to this faith and testimony – things for which to praise God; things to tell the world about His purposes of blessing, and – yes – of curse.

This brings us full circle to Asaph's conclusion, which was stated in verse 1 – what we might also call his thesis statement: "Truly God is good to Israel, to such as are pure in heart." God is good to His people. He is good in Himself. Perfectly good, faultlessly righteous, and absolutely holy. And in Psalm 73, we can see a foreshadowing of the grace of the Gospel of Jesus Christ in the New Testament (*cf.* John 3:16-21).

What Is Your Spiritual State?

Coffee-breaks can sometimes be quite revealing. In the school where I taught Biology, the science teachers were wont to gather in the Chemistry Prep Room and discuss matters of the moment over a hot drink.[31] On one occasion, a teacher came in late, all hot and bothered because some pupil, doing a survey for one of his classes, had asked her for her religious views. She told us, "I said to him that that was between me and God, and none of his business – and sent him packing!" That was the predominant attitude of the members of the church I grew up in. It was a congregation of the national Church of Scotland with maybe 1,000 names on the roll in the 1960's. I could number the serious Christians I knew on the fingers of one hand, and the minister was not one of them (I did hear many years later that he was converted, and pastoring a different church). The Bible was not studied; the Gospel was not preached; there was no conversation on spiritual things or the state of the soul; and there was nothing approaching biblical testimony-bearing, far less evangelism. It was all "be good" and lead

---

[31] I was a teacher of Biology in Trinity Academy, Edinburgh, Scotland, 1967-1970, after which I came to the USA to study for the Gospel ministry.

a decent life. Whatever "faith" people had, it was private and nobody else's business. And I, then a young Christian, concluded that they would not articulate a Christian testimony, because they could not. They were badly taught and seemed content to be so. My home church duly died, long ago, and an independent evangelical church now uses the building. Contrast this with Asaph's testimony in Psalm 73.

Out and out Unbelievers

As we have seen already, Asaph first has a general word about where all unbelief is going – unless, of course, averted by God's saving grace: "For indeed, those who are far from You shall perish..." (v. 27a). This is the downside of the basic alternatives facing sinners of mankind. As the Lord commissioned Jeremiah in a later day: "Now you shall say to this people, 'Thus says the LORD: "Behold, I set before you the way of life and the way of death."'" (Jer. 21:8). Clearly, there is in this a call to flee the wrath to come, and with it, an implicit promise of newness of life in the Lord who saves sinners who will turn to Him in faith and repentance.

We also have a word to those who were once professed followers of God – or at least thought they were – but had since decidedly gone their own way: "You have destroyed all those who have deserted You for harlotry." (v. 27b). Unbelief is called "harlotry" – this includes *practical* unbelief in a believer – because it is the radical rejection of the Redeemer and His righteousness, for whatever, or whoever, is the illicit idol we have chosen to serve. Sinners love to minimize their sins and even turn them into quasi-virtues. We will talk, on the one hand, about "mistakes," and "peccadilloes," and "sowing wild oats," and on the other, blame our "demons." The former excuses our sins as mere slips; the latter shifts the blame for things that cannot be explained away as the expected failings of normal, decent folk.

This is a stark reminder that, "It is a fearful thing to fall into the hands of the living God." (Heb. 10:31). Sin has consequences and God is surely to be feared on account of our sin – both our spiritual condition and our godless actions. The fear of God ought to attend, and hopefully turn us from, contemplated and actual sin. *Not* to take God seriously is to dismiss Him from your world and your life. It is to declare Him non-existent as far as you are concerned. And why, indeed, would you fear a non-existent god, or one who would forgive you anyway – like the man I once heard say, "God's in the business of forgiveness, isn't he?" Not *fearing* God is to deny the reality of His character and the truth of all His self-revelation. In this state, unbelievers can expect nothing but the lost eternity they mock as impossible, from the righteous Judge they dismiss as impotent, if not indeed non-existent.

Over against that, to be gripped by a foreboding apprehension of God's displeasure and possible judgment should be taken as an overture of His grace calling you immediately to "repentance toward God and faith toward our Lord Jesus Christ." (Acts 20:21). When we have heard the facts of the matter from the Lord, then "if we sin willfully after we have received the knowledge of the truth, there no longer remains a sacrifice for sins, but a certain fearful expectation of judgment, and fiery indignation which will devour the adversaries. Anyone who has rejected Moses' law dies without mercy on the testimony of two or three witnesses. Of how much worse punishment, do you suppose, will he be thought worthy who has trampled the Son of God underfoot, counted the blood of the covenant by which he was sanctified a common thing, and insulted the Spirit of grace?" (Heb. 10:26-29). If you will not fear God now, you will certainly fear Him in "the day of the Lord." (2 Pet. 3:10; Rev. 6:17). Steadfastly unrepentant sinners presume upon the grace, mercy and peace of God at their eternal risk, for He who keeps "mercy for thousands, forgiving iniquity and transgression and sin," will not be "clearing the guilty." (Exod. 34:7).

Back-slidden Believers

But what of believers in their sins? Believers are still sinners. They are not *lost* sinners, but are *saved* sinners, and nonetheless still afflicted by indwelling sin. Like Asaph and David, believers can backslide into practical sinning in very serious ways. Asaph offers a word to believers that they not dabble with the doubt and discontent that had brought him so low. As we have seen already, it is an honest, sound, personal, experiential, intimate and God-centered account, and an open, public witness to what ailed him and how he was healed. It is about the most vital issues of life, in time and eternity. Solomon later lays this upon our consciences: "Keep your heart with all diligence, for out of it spring the issues of life." (Prov. 4:23).

We should remember that believers – who have come to know the love of the Lord as their Savior – can only have a greater sensitivity to sin than the as yet unconverted – and the determined reprobates – of this world.

Finally ... A word to you in whichever may be your true spiritual condition today.[32]

1. To those who are *not seeking* – and may never have sought – to draw near to God, the Lord appeals to you to "Draw near to Him and He will draw near to you." (Jas. 4:8). Charles Simeon pleads with those who are saying to the Lord, in their hearts, "Depart from us, for we do not desire the knowledge of Your ways." (Job 21:14): "O that you might tremble at the denunciations of his wrath. And not bring upon yourselves the bitter experience of it in the eternal world."[33] In our (New Testament) times, this means coming to Jesus Christ. He is calling you in His Gospel to believe upon Him and be saved (Acts 16:31), specifically assuring you that, "if you confess with your mouth the Lord Jesus and believe in your heart that God has raised Him from the dead, you will be saved." (Rom. 10:9).

2. To those who "draw near," but only *outwardly*, the Lord warns you of the danger of the many who "draw near to Me with their mouth, and honor Me with their lips, but their heart is far from Me." – And further explains, "in vain they worship Me, teaching as doctrines the commandments of men." (Matt. 15:8-9). The writer to the Hebrews encourages you with the powerful assertion, "how much more shall the blood of Christ, who through the eternal Spirit offered Himself without spot to God, cleanse your conscience from dead works to serve the living God?" (Heb. 9:14). Will you not respond by opening your heart to Christ, trusting and resting upon Him as your Savior?

3. To those who have formerly professed to believe in and follow after Jesus, but are doubting Him and are tempted to wander away from Him – and may already have drawn away from Him in particular ways – God is calling, in words through the prophet Jeremiah, "Return, you backsliding children, And I will heal your backslidings." (Jer. 3:22). The Lord had earlier promised His people, "Return, backsliding Israel, ... I will not cause My anger to fall on you. For I am merciful, ... I will not remain angry forever." (Jer. 3:12; *cf.* 35:15). The Lord is *not* saying,

---

[32] I am here indebted to Charles Simeon for the challenge of his exposition of Psalm 73:28 in his *Expository Outlines*, Vol. 6:22-23.

[33] C. Simeon, *op. cit.*, Vol. 6:22.

however, that doubters, complainers, backsliders and rebellious professors of faith can console themselves with the easy assurance that "God still loves me and it will all pan out well in the end." The basic fact is that sinning negates personal assurance, and sinning sinners, saved or unsaved, have no right to say "God loves me anyway" and move on. God is clear on this score: "If anyone does not abide in Me, he is cast out as a branch and is withered; and they gather them and throw them into the fire, and they are burned." (John 15:6). His promise will not be fulfilled in the case of those who will not repent and return to Him. He presses this home to the church in the most trenchant warning of the consequences of denying his promises in the Word: "Nevertheless I have this against you, that you have left your first love. 'Remember therefore from where you have fallen; repent and do the first works, or else I will come to you quickly and remove your lampstand from its place – unless you repent.'" (Rev. 2:4-5). No one has a right to feel assured of the love of God when *in the act and state* of denying (hating?) Him by *actually and willfully sinning*! Sin can only "justify" fearing God (and hopefully will engender true repentance). Only Gospel grace in Christ, sincere heart-love from and in Christ, can "cast out fear" as *per* 1 John 4:18. True experience of assurance cannot survive sinning and can only revive with the exercise of true repentance and faith.

But bear in mind that the fear of God is a work of God's Spirit in our hearts and should be received as a wakeup call not only to the unconverted, but also to the backsliding believers, recalling them to love God and keep His commandments. In this sense, the fear of God will be a component in the extension of God's loving purpose in Christ to dead souls He will make alive. That however does not make the sin less potentially deadly, or the fear of God less fearful. Only the embrace and application of the perfect love of God in Christ – our love is never perfect outside of Glory, after all – will see that fear defanged and its terrors cast out (*cf.* 1 John 4:18).[34]

---

[34] There are of course degrees of fear, and not a few converts to Christ may have but little fear when converted to Christ, as indeed may many backsliders when they are restored to fellowship with the Lord. Believers who fall into serious sin are bound to be more sensitive to sin when overtaken in a fault later in life – see the Apostle Paul in Romans 7:21-25 and the glorious conclusion of the verses that follow.

4. To those who find real joy in communion with the Lord and in the obedience of faith: is it not true that "our fellowship is with God, and with His Son Jesus Christ." (1 John 1:3)? William McEwen observes of the sincere and sound believer: "In times of temptation he preserves his integrity, because of the fear of God: in times of danger he is confident: when sinners in Zion are afraid, and fearfulness surprises the hypocrite, he fears indeed, but with that filial fear which is the daughter of faith, the sister of love, the mother of obedience, and the beginning of wisdom [Prov. 9:10]."[35] Charles Simeon of Cambridge exhorts us: "Continue then and increase your diligence in walking with God. Then you shall not only say *now*, 'It is good for me to draw nigh to God;' but you shall one day add with ten-fold emphasis, 'It is good for me to have drawn nigh to God.' Yes; if *now* you can look back upon your seasons of communion with God as the best and happiest hours of your life, much more shall you, when your fellowship with him shall be more immediate, and you are dwelling in the very bosom of your God."[36]

"Therefore we also, since we are surrounded by so great a cloud of witnesses, let us lay aside every weight, and the sin which so easily ensnares us, and let us run with endurance the race that is set before us, looking unto Jesus, the author and finisher of our faith, who for the joy that was set before Him endured the cross, despising the shame, and has sat down at the right hand of the throne of God. For consider Him who endured such hostility from sinners against Himself, lest you become weary and discouraged in your souls." (Heb. 12:1-3).

"Therefore humble yourselves under the mighty hand of God, that He may exalt you in due time, casting all your care upon Him, for He cares for you." (1 Pet. 5:6-7). "Truly God is good to Israel, to such as are pure in heart." (Psalm 73:1; cf. Matthew 5:8; Galatians 6:16).

---

[35] William McEwen, *Select Essays*. No. 44: "Reverence and Godly Fear" (1834 ed.).
[36] C. Simeon, *op. cit.*, Vol. 6:23.

PUBLICATIONS BY THE AUTHOR

Available from Crown & Covenant, 7418 Penn Avenue, Pittsburgh, PA 15208:
- *Ten Words from God (an exposition of the Ten Commandments)*
- *Portraits of Christ* (with David G. Whitla)
- *Prayers of the Bible: 366 Devotionals to encourage your Prayer Life.*
- *Christ's Covenant and Your Life.*
- *Redemption, Reconciliation, and Reformation: the Shorter Writings of Alexander McLeod, D.D., 1802-1833*, edited by Gordon J. Keddie.
- *Political Danger: Essays on the Mediatorial Kingship of Christ over nations and their political institutions, 1809-1838*, (The shorter writings of James Renwick Willson, D.D., edited by Gordon J. Keddie)

Available from Reformation Heritage Books, 3070 29th St SE, Grand Rapids, MI 49512:
- *William McEwen: The Glory and Fullness of Jesus Christ*, edited by Gordon J. Keddie (First published in 1763 as *"Grace and Truth"*).

Available from 10ofthose, 900 East Jefferson Street, La Grange, KY 40031. Phone: (502) 265-0492. (All published by Evangelical Press, Darlington, England).
- *John: An EP Study Commentary*, 2 Vols.
- *You are my Witnesses. (A Welwyn Commentary - on the Book of Acts)*
- *According to Promise (A Welwyn Commentary on the book of Numbers).*
- *Triumph of the King (A Welwyn Series Commentary on 2 Samuel).*
- *The Practical Christian (A Welwyn Series Commentary on the Epistle of James).*
- *Dawn of a Kingdom (A Welwyn Series Commentary on 1 Samuel).*
- *Preacher on the Run. (A Welwyn Series Commentary on Jonah).*
- *The Lord is His Name (A Welwyn Series Commentary on Amos).*
- *Even in Darkness, (A Welwyn Series Commentary on Judges and Ruth).*

Available from Wipf and Stock, 199 West 8th Avenue Suite 3, Eugene, OR:
- *He Spoke in Parables (An exposition of the Parables of Jesus).*
- *Looking for the Good Life (An exposition of the Book of Ecclesiastes).*